A PASSION FOR GARLIC

A PASSION FOR GARLIC

Penny Drinkwater

and

Elaine Self

There is no herb, nor weed, but God has
given virtue to them, to help man.
Andrew Boorde, 1542

Duckworth

First published in 1980 by
Gerald Duckworth & Co. Ltd
The Old Piano Factory
43 Gloucester Crescent, London NW1

ISBN 0 7156 1404 5 cloth
0 7156 1405 3 paper

British Library Cataloguing in Publication Data

Drinkwater, Penny
 A passion for garlic.
 1. Cookery (Garlic)
 I. Title   II. Self, Elaine
 641.6'5'26   TX819.G3

 ISBN 0–7156–1404–5
 ISBN 0–7156–1405–3 Pbk.

Typeset by Computacomp (UK) Ltd, Fort William, Scotland.
Printed in Great Britain by Redwood Burn Limited
Trowbridge & Esher

CONTENTS

Garlic (gāulĭɛk). [OE. *gárléāc*] (f. *gár* spear + *léac*
leek). 1. A plant of the genus *Allium* (usu. *A.
sativum*) having a bulbous root, a very strong
smell, and an acrid, pungent taste. †2. Name
of a jig or farce – 1630. 1. Clove of g. 2). Oil of
g., an essential oil obtained from the bulb
and stem of g. Hence Garlicky *a.* savouring
or smelling of g.

Passion (pæ∫an) … a commanding,
vehement, or overpowering feeling …

ACKNOWLEDGMENTS

We have been helped by dozens of interested bystanders – a few standing well back – during the period of our obsession with garlic. Our first thanks are due to the cultural attachés and culinary enthusiasts of the many countries represented in the cookery section of this book, and to the restaurateurs and wine merchants who were generous with their assistance (a passion for garlic is all the better for being shared), as follows:

The Wine Development Board, Hugh McKay and the Italian Institute for Foreign Trade, the Euro Import Export Company, the Soviet Embassy, VI Lenin All-Union Academy of Agricultural Science of Lenin Order, Embajada de Mexico, the Spanish Embassy, the Spanish Citrus Management Committee, the Press Section of the Hungarian Embassy, Food and Wine from France, F. Rochias et Cie, J. Hennessy & Co., Comité Interprofessionel du Vin de Champagne, Champneys at Tring, Paxton & Whitfield Ltd., The Cape Wine Centre, The Good Housekeeping Institute, Roddy Hooper, Michael Jacobson, Gela Peters, Gerald Asher, David Wolfe, Miguel Torres of Penedes, Miss P. Green of French Wine Farmers, the Cultural and Information Office, Brazilian Embassy, Andrea's Continental Restaurant, the Bombay Restaurant, Mr. Chung of Pang's, and Liz Fronczek of The Tate Gallery Restaurant – all of London. And the British Duck Advisory Bureau of Poulter House, Leeds.

Thanks are due also to the librarians of many societies and institutions who were both helpful and generous. Librarians have what the homeopathic medical world might call 'garlic personalities', for whenever we mentioned our quest their eyes lit up and they were off like arrows into the arcane world of the specialist. We would also like to thank our correspondents in Great Britain and the United States and on the Continent for their kindness in replying to questions, especially D. S. Backhouse, Dr. Hans Reuter and Derek Senior.

Families and friends have borne the brunt of our preoccupation. They have allowed meal after meal to feature the beloved plant and with docile good will have even submitted their coughs and sore throats to our experimentation. To all of them we extend our loving thanks.

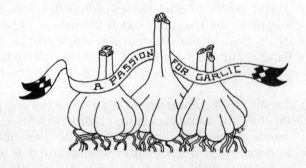

viii

INTRODUCTION

When Satan stepped out of the Garden of Eden,
after the fall of Man, garlic sprang from the spot
where he placed his left foot, and onion from that
where his right foot touched.
                              Mohammedan legend

Our Apothecary's shop is our garden full of pot-
herbs, and our Doctor is a clove of garlic.
                              A Deep Snow, 1615

A necklace of garlic keeps vampires away.
                              Traditional

Garlic in food is delicious – *garlic* is delicious. Its greatest quality is that it
performs magic upon the simplest ingredients in the world – upon
bread, and tomatoes, beans and lettuce, chicken and lamb. Garlic turns
basic foods into masterpieces. No other plant enhances the ordinary as
garlic does, and none can so transform and illuminate commonplace
foods, making of them splendidly different national dishes.

Garlic can work culinary miracles. You can use it by the handful to
make a classic French soup – Tourain à l'Ail, wonderfully fragrant, yet
composed of ingredients always at hand. Or in minute quantities,
rubbing a clove around the inside of a wooden salad bowl. The Israelis
make an instant garlic-blessed salad with plain broad beans; and the
Chinese make a succulent beef dish using crushed garlic in a simple
sauce.

Garlic must be one of the oldest cultivated plants in existence –
fragments of a garlic-like plant were unearthed when Jericho was
excavated, and indeed there is evidence that it existed even earlier. It has

1

been known, and used, for thousands of years, from pre-dynastic Egypt through the histories of Greece and Rome, from Old Testament times to yesterday in the apothecary's physick garden and today in the kitchens of good cooks the world over.

Garlic has had a curious history, unlike that of any other plant we know. For a long time it was viewed with contempt as food for peasants and slaves, but it has also been praised as the greatest flavouring ever discovered by man. It has been used in the quiet domestic world of folk medicine as a sovereign remedy for almost all the ills that flesh is heir to, whether as an antiseptic or a hopeful aphrodisiac, and contemporary medical research, as we shall see, takes some of these claims seriously. Famous as a charm against evil spirits, especially vampires, garlic has also been called the ruination of good friendships, good love affairs and, worst of all, good food.

Allium sativum – cultivated garlic – probably originated in the steppes of Central Asia, where it grew wild. It is possible that the Crusaders first brought it to the West. We know it travelled westward, first to the countries around the Mediterranean, to Egypt and Africa, and then to the rest of Europe and the British Isles. India, China and Japan have known and cultivated it – for food and as a medicine – for at least a thousand years.

In 450 B.C. Herodotus said that the ancient Egyptians had worshipped garlic and that it was inscribed on their pyramids in a list of the payments made to the workmen who built them. Today historians think that Herodotus was wrong, and that Greek travellers had misinterpreted certain tomb paintings which depicted the garlic plant lying among other offerings on a table near a shrine: not a God to be worshipped, but gifts for the Gods. Nor is there any proof that it was given in wages – the Egyptians, apparently, did not carve their building costs on their monuments. Still, the Roman poet Juvenal used the tale to make a joke about the Egyptians which has lasted for centuries: the Egyptians worship garlic, and swear oaths upon it. Garlic and the smell of garlic entered the lists early as a subject for humour.

But if the Egyptians did not worship garlic, they did put clay models of garlic bulbs into their cemeteries as long ago as 5000 B.C. These were found by archaeologists in the 1920s, in Naqada; they were made with great skill, the cloves attached to a flattened base, just as they grow in life. The whole bulb, painted white, looked very like the real thing.

Not models in clay, but the bulbs themselves were put into the tomb of King Tut-ankh-Amon in 1500 B.C. You can see these petrified bulbs in the National Museum in Cairo, looking not very different from the garlic available today at the corner greengrocer's. They may have been

2

put into the King's tomb for food, or as offerings to the Gods, or to keep away evil spirits.

Horace's Third Epode sums up his feelings about 'that wicked garlic' when Maecenas served it to him at dinner:

> What venom is this that rages in my frame? Has viper's blood without my knowledge been brewed into these herbs? ... If ever, my merry Maecenas, you wish to repeat the jest, I pray your sweetheart may put her hands before your kisses, and lie on the farthest edge of the couch.

In short, not a suitable food for a Roman citizen.

The Romans, then, for the most part spurned garlic in their cookery – we are not told whether merry Maecenas had a taste for it himself. But Pliny said it could cure 61 different ailments; it was acceptable as a medicine if not as a food. The Romans also gave it to their soldiers as a tonic, to give them courage before battle; and they also fed it to their fighting cocks, with the same intention. They forced their criminals to eat it, to purge them of their crimes; and it was put under cairns of stones at crossroads as an offering to Hecate.

Garlic was a staple in the diet of the poor; and when the Roman legions came to Britain, they brought garlic with them.

Garlic appears in the earliest known recipe for salad, written in English and dated 1393: 'Take parsley, sage, and garlic, chibols, onions, leek, borage, mints.' Garlic was much appreciated in medieval England, but the Elizabethans thought less well of it and it gradually fell out of favour. It came to be known as 'the poor man's physic, of special value to seafaring men because it pacifieth the disposition to vomit' – and seasickness was added to the long list of ailments for which it was already believed to be the cure. By the seventeenth century, garlic was no longer acceptable in court circles, or in cultivated society. During the next 200 years, it retired to the cottage garden – an old wives' remedy and the herbalist's cure-all.

By the nineteenth century, garlic had virtually disappeared from English tables, so that Mrs Beeton could suggest that no more than the smallest end of one clove was quite sufficient to flavour any salad.

In the New World it fared rather better. The Indians of North America already knew a wild meadow garlic; they used the crushed bulbs to relieve the pain of insect stings, discovered that garlic could prevent and cure scurvy, and that the bulbs could be boiled and eaten. When America opened her doors to mass immigration in the nineteenth century, the Spanish, Italians and Jews came with their native cuisines; garlic was used in the cookery of all these ethnic groups. But gradually, as in England, it ceased to be an acceptable food; to smell of garlic was thought to be 'vulgar', and for a long time, in a country where assimilation was the goal of all, he who smelled of garlic had to bear the opprobrious title of 'greenhorn'.

What has happened to change this gloomy picture?

In England, the cooks who only obeyed Mrs Beeton's more pallid dicta, and who served the results to docile employers, abruptly disappeared. But after the Second World War, the servantless middle classes, adrift in their unfamiliar kitchens, began by trying to imitate the formal meals to which they were accustomed. The results were sometimes disastrous. Then, almost overnight, it dawned on them that they were free. Travel to Italy, France and Spain, formerly open only to poets and the rich, completed the revolution, and food with savour, and flavour, prepared with loving skill (and glorious garlic) began to appear upon formerly timid tables.

At first there was perhaps an overemphasis upon imitating the foreign – there were too many inferior 'daubes' when a careful attention to the excellencies of good traditional British foods would have been preferable. But a balance was soon struck, and today there are few domestic cooks in England who are unaware of the advantages of combining 'the best of British' with the newer importations from the Continent. The results are splendid.

Almost the same thing happened in the United States, where the servant girls disappeared after the war into factories and office jobs. Then people remembered the fragrant pasta sauce kept simmering on grandmother's coal stove, and the succulent chicken with rice they had tasted on holiday in Mexico, and garlic soups, and pork with sauerkraut, the sausages and stews – all those aromatic delights had almost been lost in the scramble to be all-American. Then, as in England, good food, cooked with imagination and flair, began to reappear in American homes.

Of course it would be an exaggeration to suggest that garlic as a seasoning was totally neglected during those dark years of wretched domestic cookery. In fact there were always pockets of interest in it – witness the garlic sauces and pickles of the mid-nineteenth century, and the Victorian gentlefolk's enthusiasm for 'devils' (we include one or two; they are due for a revival) and for such everyday piquant mixtures as Worcestershire Sauce.

Nor was it forgotten by the cottage healers and the herbal physicians; they continued to prescribe garlic to their patients during the long years when to smell of it put one beyond the pale in polite society.

Wonderful qualities lie beneath the skin of the garlic clove. It is an

4

essential ingredient if we are to enjoy the best of the world's cookery, and of increasing interest to scientists in the world of medicine and healing – a safe plant medicine whose ability to cure has already been proved. A fascinating plant with a long history, we have not yet learned the extent of its usefulness and power.

And of course, it also protects us against those vampires.

Part I

Garlic throughout the World

Garlic Recipes

'Happiness and peace begin, geographically, where garlic is used in cooking.' Thus did the great Marcel Boulestin pontificate – and how right he was.

Our recipes come for the most part from those countries where garlic flourishes – both the tame and the wild. Cooler countries tend to use garlic sparingly in their cuisines, and warmer ones with more abandon, but very few countries entirely ignore its virtues. Some of the recipes are ancient and some are new. A few have originated in one country and moved to another, subtly changing during the journey. Most of the recipes are the favourites of passionate garlic lovers and all can be easily made at home for only one or two require ingredients difficult to procure.

Garlic can be used aggressively, as in the Italian peasant's *pano al pomidoro*, doorstep slabs of bread liberally pasted with tomato and garlic; or as in *Bistecca Pizzaiola*, an oven-baked steak with a pulsating garlic and tomato sauce; or again, as in Spain's *Zazuela de Mariscos*, a massive selection of fishes, first lightly fried and then finished with a gutsy garlic and onion sauce.

Garlic can be used subtly, as the Indians and Chinese use it; or frugally, as do the English, or gourmet-style, as do the French.

Countries round the Mediterranean throw caution to the winds and use garlic in vast quantities, while a four-season country like Hungary uses it intriguingly but modestly.

Garlic can be, and is often, eaten raw. It can be used as a condiment, as in garlic salt or garlic powder. Or you can rub peeled garlic gently round a salad bowl, insert a sliver or two into (or under) the Sunday roast, or with the juices extracted by a garlic squeezer or press, introduce a delicate flavour into cottage pie or casserole.

Garlic must be fresh and crisp when you cut into it; nothing tastes worse than garlic which is beginning to spoil. When you are cooking it

9

in an open pan or skillet, be brief: garlic blackens and burns quickly, and the smell and taste of burnt garlic does not give pleasure. If it is used lavishly – and it must often be so – chop the cloves incredibly fine, almost to a molecular state. In this way the flavour becomes part of the orchestral whole, not a dominating note. If the garlic ever becomes overpowering, chew a stalk of parsley, one of the traditional antidotes, and rub your fingers with lemon juice to remove the odour.

On the banks of the Loire, they chop the green leaves of garlic and eat them in salads, while the cloves are eaten with fresh cheese. In the East, they use garlic powder as a substitute for pepper. There are garlic powders and garlic pieces and garlic salts for sale, but the purist, the true lover, will have nothing less than the head or bulb itself. You can buy them singly or in cellophane – boxed in pairs or trios – or in net bags of two or three; but the ideal way is to invest in a whole string of garlic. At the Osmans in the Fulham Palace Road in London, they lay such strings out in rows, a glorious sight for the garlic lover. Theirs are French, and a string of garlic, composed of the heads entwined with garlic leaf and straw, is an aesthetic addition to any kitchen. A string stores well and will last you for two or three months, so it is not a wasteful buy.

Which is the fairest garlic of them all? Our greengrocer says 'the French', but every kind has its champions, some praising the Spanish, others the Italian. A director of the London wine firm John Harvey & Sons swears that Korean garlic is the strongest. What about home-grown garlic? It is perfectly feasible to grow your own in backyard garden or window-box herb collection.

Finally, it is worth reflecting that not only do different countries treat their garlic differently – sometimes as a seasoning, more positively as a herb, or dynamically as a vegetable in its own right – but also attitudes in any country can change as the centuries spin by. In Chaucer's England they were told to 'peel bulbs of garlic, plunge in pot with water and oil, and boil, and further season with saffron, salt and strong powder' – not a recipe with much appeal for us today.

But here are dozens of new delights – new ways to use one of our oldest cultivated plants, and new recipes to alter the world's 'geography' and bring you happiness and peace.

Boulestin, wise man, was right.

TABLE OF EQUIVALENT TEMPERATURES

	Gas radiation and regulo mark	Electric temperature
Cool	$\frac{1}{4}$–$\frac{1}{2}$	230° F
Very Slow	1	250° F
Slow	2	325° F
Very Moderate	3	350° F
Moderate	4	375° F
Moderately Hot	5	400° F
Fairly Hot	6	425° F
Hot	7	450° F
Extremely Hot	8–9	500°–550° F

TABLE OF CONVERSIONS

USA measures	Imperial measures (solids – meat, vegetables, rice, etc.)	Metric measures
$\frac{1}{8}$ cup	1 oz	25 g
$\frac{1}{4}$ cup	2 oz	50 g
$\frac{1}{2}$ cup	4 oz	100–125 g
$\frac{3}{4}$ cup	6 oz	175 g
1 cup	8 oz	225 g

FLUIDS

US:	8 fl oz	= 1 cup	= $\frac{1}{2}$ pt	US:	32 fl oz	= 1 qt
GB:	10 fl oz	= 1 cup	= $\frac{1}{2}$ pt	GB:	Not commonly used, but contains	
US:	16 fl oz	= 2 cups	= 1 pt		40 fl oz	= 1 qt
GB:	20 fl oz	= 2 cups	= 1 pt			

1 fl oz = 25 ml
2 fl oz = 50 ml
5 fl oz = 150 ml
10 fl oz = 300 ml
15 fl oz = 450 ml
20 fl oz = 600 ml = British pint
35 fl oz = 1 litre = 3 fl oz more than US quart

When using metric measures, instead of a teaspoon use a 5-ml spoon and instead of a tablespoon use a 15-ml spoon.

11

ARGENTINA

There is nothing subtle about most Argentinian food. A prosperous South American country, Argentina produces and exports a great deal of garlic and enormous quantities of beef. Few cuisines can match the lusty pampas tradition.

· The *Carbonada* is a dish for a gigantic party, or you can reduce the quantities for a smaller company. The combination of fruit and meat is an unusual one, and the garlic enhances all the flavours.

As for the *Locro de trigo*, it is an extremely popular and warming winter stew; the garlic is in the sauce this time. We can hardly imagine serving it to less than fifteen hardy souls; but again, try cutting down the quantities for an unusual supper dish.

Carbonada Criolla

You will need a large, cast-iron pot with a well-fitting lid to make this dish properly.

Ingredients

½ cup vegetable oil
1 large onion, chopped
6 cloves garlic, chopped
1 pound can tomatoes
2 lbs beef, cut into cubes
a piece of beef marrow, if available
bouquet garni (marjoram, parsley, bay leaf – or a ready-made one)
¾ cup butter
1 carrot, chopped

2 pts beef stock
1 sweet potato, peeled and cut into dice
4 white potatoes, peeled and cut into dice
the kernels from 3 ears of fresh corn, or 1 can corn kernels
½ lb green peas
1 lb long grain rice
1 can peach halves

Method

Lightly fry the onion and garlic in the vegetable oil. Add the beef and cook quickly on a high heat. Add the tomatoes, the bouquet garni and salt and pepper to taste. Cook for two minutes, then add the butter, the carrot and the stock. Cover with the lid and cook slowly until the meat is tender. Then add the beef marrow and both kinds of potatoes. Bring the mixture to the boil and add the rice, corn, peas, and the syrup from the peaches. Arrange the peaches on top and cover the pan tightly. Cook until the rice is done, about 20 minutes. The final consistency should be thick but juicy, so add more stock if necessary.

Locro de trigo

Ingredients

1 pound wheat grains
6 pts water plus 4 cups cold water
2 lbs beefsteak cut into pieces
beef bones
1 lb tripe, cut into pieces
1 lb sausages
1 lb haricot or navy beans, cooked

until tender and then mashed with a fork
½ lb bacon
for the sauce: 1 tablespoon lard, 1 onion, 6 cloves garlic, 1 red pepper, salt and pepper

Method

In a large saucepan bring the 6 pints of water to the boil, add the wheat grains and reheat the water. Just before it begins to boil, add the 4 cups of cold water. Continue to cook very slowly until the wheat grains have opened. Now sauté the pieces of beefsteak in a little oil until they have lost their red colour. Add the meat and the bones to the water in the saucepan, then add the tripe and the sausages, which you have also sautéed briefly, the bacon and the beans. Cook on a very low heat, stirring occasionally. When the meat is completely tender remove the beef bones, make the sauce, and add it to the stew.

To make the sauce: In the lard, slowly fry the onion and garlic chopped together, stir in the red pepper which you have deseeded and diced, and season with salt and pepper. Add the mixture to the stew when the sauce is thick.

13

BRAZIL

Brazil, the giant of South America, occupies half the continent and although there is, as the jingle insists, an awful lot of coffee in Brazil, there is also a great deal of garlic. The cuisine is robust and fully flavoured. The traditional recipe for *Peru à Brasiliera* calls for two stuffings; we give you just one – the second is a bread stuffing made with bacon and onions. This is an unusual way of roasting turkey: the flavour is excellent.

Peru à Brasiliera
(Turkey Brazilian style)

Ingredients

1 roasting turkey, about 8–10 lbs

Marinade of the following items:
3 garlic cloves pounded to a paste
black pepper/salt
1 clove
½ cup chopped celery

1 chopped onion
½ cup chopped parsley
1 grated carrot
2 cups white wine
1 cup wine vinegar

Method

Marinate the turkey in this *Vinha d'Alho*, or marinade, overnight, turning once or twice, but allowing the breast of the bird to remain in the liquid longer than the back. Next day, cook the giblets in water with salt, celery and parsley. When they are tender, remove from the water and chop finely. Now make a stuffing with the following ingredients:

chopped onion
parsley
half the chopped giblets (or, if making only one stuffing, add all the giblets)
4–5 drops Tabasco sauce

4 cups Manioc meal (if unavailable, use a fine cereal like Farina, or finely crushed rusks or water biscuits or soda crackers)
½ cup stuffed olives
3 chopped hard boiled eggs

14

Method

Cook the chopped onion in butter in an open pan, add the rest of the ingredients, mix well and stuff the bird. Roast, basting with marinade and melted butter, in the usual manner – medium heat, 25 minutes to the pound, plus 20 minutes over.

Carne Ensopada
(Brazilian Pot Roast)

Ingredients

rump roast of beef, about 4 lbs
(Trim off as much of the fat as possible.)
2 oz ham and 2 oz bacon, chopped together

½ cup wine vinegar
1 teaspoon salt pounded with
1 garlic clove
1 grated onion

Method

Lard the beef with the mixture of ham and bacon – make small incisions and stuff the mixture in them. Now marinate the beef in the next four ingredients for 2 hours. Wipe the beef and sear it on all sides in a heavy saucepan. Pour off any fat, add the marinade, cover the saucepan tightly and cook the meat over a low heat for about 2 hours.

Liver Marinade

Ingredients

1 lb beef liver thinly sliced
clove garlic, crushed
pepper and salt

¼ pt wine vinegar
2 large onions
freshly cooked rice

Method

Arrange liver slices in a shallow dish and pour over the wine vinegar to which you have added the garlic and seasonings. Marinate for several hours. Slice the onions and fry them quickly in hot fat until they are brown. Remove and keep them hot. Pour off the marinade, strain it and heat in the same pan. Add the liver and cook it quickly. Add the onions, reheat, and arrange the mixture over the rice.

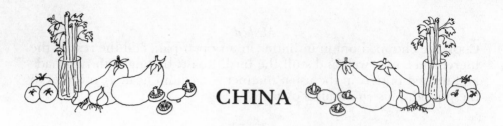

CHINA

China is vast, its cuisine various. In Chinese cookery, elaborate preparations are completed before swift and simple cooking processes begin. The final results are always fragrant and lovely to look at. The Chinese cook uses the blunt edge of the cleaver not only to agitate and break the skin of the clove in order to peel it, but also to crush the clove totally.

Garlic is particularly characteristic of the cooking in Peking and the north of China. It is grown in commune gardens as a vegetable and a seasoning – and for medicinal use as well.

Macao Prawns

Ingredients

1 lb cooked prawns (or ¾ lb frozen prawns)
salt, finely ground black pepper
3 tablespoons butter
4 cloves garlic, chopped
1 green pepper, deseeded and chopped
4 tomatoes, peeled and cut into quarters
½ cup black olives, stoned

Method

Season the prawns with salt and pepper and set aside while you prepare the sauce. Melt the butter gently in a heavy skillet and cook the garlic and green pepper in it. When they have softened, add the tomatoes and olives, keeping the heat low. Simmer gently for 10 minutes, then add the prawns. Serve with plain boiled rice.

Sze-Chuen Chili Soya Beef

Ingredients

2 peeled garlic cloves
1 fresh red chili
1 tsp black soya bean paste
vegetable oil
4 oz uncooked beef, cut into
julienne strips
pinch sugar
teaspoon sesame oil
2 spring onions (scallions) very finely sliced

16

Pound garlic and chili together in pestle and mortar. Add soya bean paste and blend. Fry this compound paste until golden in very hot oil for a few seconds. In another pan, fry beef in hot oil for 20 seconds and remove with perforated spoon. Now add the meat to the fried paste. Season with sugar and blend in the sesame oil. Just before serving, add the finely sliced onions. Very hot!

Garlic Compoy (Peking)

This recipe calls for an irresistible amount of garlic, but we don't seriously expect you to make it: compoy costs £40 a pound in Chinese supermarkets. You might like to use another dried salted fish although of course the result would be entirely different.

Ingredients

4 oz compoy (dried, salted scallops)
5 whole garlic heads
2 teaspoons rice wine
2 pinches salt

½ teaspoon sugar
prime soup (this is a soup of chicken bones and pork spare ribs boiled together for an hour)

Method
Soak compoy in water for an hour, drain, and fry in oil until it just begins to colour. Arrange the ingredients in a double boiler as follows: first the garlic cloves, peeled, then the compoy, then sprinkle on the wine, sugar and salt. Add a small quantity of the soup (about 2 tablespoons). Cover the pan closely and cook over boiling water for at least three hours. This makes a sauce to serve with rice.

Shanghai Eel

Ingredients

6 tablespoons vegetable oil
8 oz eel fillets, cut to the thickness of a chopstick and the length of a toothpick
3 tsp soya sauce
a sprinkling of sugar

1 tsp fresh ginger root, shredded finely
a sprinkling of rice wine
freshly ground pepper
2 finely chopped garlic cloves

17

Method

Heat half the oil and cook the eel in it briefly. Now add the soya sauce, sugar, ginger, wine and pepper. Stir-fry for one or two minutes. Pile up in a mound and make a hole in the centre. Put the chopped garlic in the hole. Heat the rest of the oil until just smoking and pour over the garlic. Serve immediately. The Chinese use yellow eel, but ordinary eel is an acceptable substitute.

A Dip for Prawns

Ingredients

4 fl oz dark soya sauce (sweeter than ordinary)
1 fl oz ordinary soya sauce
5 fl oz vegetable oil
2–3 finely sliced garlic cloves

a fresh green chili, deseeded and finely sliced
scant teaspoon sugar
teaspoon fresh ginger, shredded

Method

Heat the oil and throw in the garlic slices. Cook until they are almost golden and crisp. Add the rest of the ingredients, mixing well. Ginger and garlic are a magical combination. Serve the dip hot but not boiling. Enough for 1 pint of prawns.

Lo-Teng Chicken

(a Cantonese dish … Canton is famous for the quality of its chickens)

Ingredients

1 whole chicken
vegetable oil
2 peeled cloves of garlic
6 oz black soya beans, previously soaked in water, and cooked
½ oz Chinese wine – Shao Lsinghuateow – (rice wine) – dry

sherry can be substituted
½ tsp sugar
dash pepper
1 tsp sesame oil
4 tablespoons hot water
½ tsp cornflour

Method

Chop the chicken into 'bite' size pieces (bones and flesh together, the Chinese way). Fry chicken in oil until just golden. Put aside. Fry garlic cloves and black soya beans in hot oil 10–20 seconds – add 4 tablespoons of water. Add chicken pieces. Add wine, sugar and pepper. Cover, and cook slowly for 15 minutes. Add sesame oil and the cornflour, dissolved in cold water. Stir, cook and serve.

N.B. Additional water and longer cooking ensures greater tenderness.

Tripe Cantonese Style

Ingredients

1 lb cooked tripe cut into thin strips
2 oz sesame oil
2 onions, chopped
2 cloves garlic, chopped

1 tablespoon dry sherry
½ pt water
1 tablespoon soya sauce
4 mushrooms, sliced
2 tomatoes, peeled and sliced

Method

Fry the tripe in the oil with the onions and garlic. Add the sherry, water, soya sauce, mushrooms and tomatoes. Simmer for half an hour and serve hot.

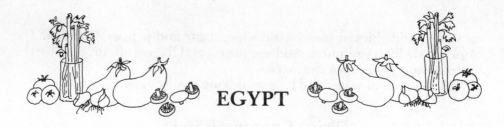

EGYPT

In Egypt the best garlic is grown in Minia and Assiut, both in the nothern part of the country. Garlic has been cultivated there since pre-dynastic times.

Egypt grows and uses a lot of garlic, and exports a great deal as well. 1978 was considered a poor year – 25 per cent less than usual was exported – but even so the Egyptians sent abroad 12,000 tons of fresh garlic, 380 tons of dehydrated garlic, and 2 tons of garlic oil.

Dehydrated garlic and garlic oil are used within the country in food production: in canneries for making tinned soups, to preserve meats and as a flavouring. One drop of the highly concentrated Egyptian garlic oil is enough to make a room uninhabitable. Pectin is extracted from the tasteless peel of the garlic cloves.

The Egyptians use garlic liberally in their cooking. Almost invariably they crush and fry the cloves before use, which does seem to make it less objectionable socially. This is how they make 'salsa tamatem', the sauce in which almost all vegetables are cooked: garlic and onion, both finely minced, are fried together, then tomato paste or freshly sieved tomatoes are added and the mixture is cooked until it becomes dark red. Vegetables are either pre-cooked, then heated in this sauce, or water or stock are added to the sauce and the vegetables are cooked in it.

Tahena 'Salad'

Method

This is really a dip made by adding 6 cloves of crushed garlic to a cup of tahena. Tahena is made with sesame paste, nut oil and a teaspoon of finely crushed cumin seeds, plus a few drops of water and the same amount of vinegar or lemon juice (or both). Beat all these ingredients together. The tahena is hard to mix at first but gradually it turns into an oyster-white sauce – eventually the consistency should be like custard or cream. The amount of garlic and cumin you then add to the tahena depends upon taste. Sometimes a little nut oil is poured over a dish of tahena 'salad' and everyone dips the local bread into it. Tahena can also be eaten with pickles, salads and any Mediterranean *mezzi*. It is a good partner to pre-dinner drinks, and excellent with traditionally grilled kebabs.

Basterma

Method

Basically, this is a raw fillet of beef which is thickly coated all over with a mixture of halba (a pungent herb) and pounded garlic, plus salt and other spices. The fillet is then allowed to stand for several hours. To serve, the coating of herbs is removed and the meat is cut into very thin slices, like raw ham. It is either eaten raw, with tomatoes and salad greens, or in sandwiches; or it is fried in ghee (clarified butter) with eggs – a sort of Egyptian ham and eggs.

Omani Aubergine

A recipe from the Sultanate of Oman

Ingredients

1 medium-to-large aubergine
olive oil
2 small tubs of yoghurt

4 cloves of garlic, crushed
salt to taste

Method

Slice the aubergine and fry the slices in olive oil until they are tender. Drain on kitchen paper. Arrange the slices of aubergine in a serving dish. Mix the garlic with the yoghurt and add salt to taste. Pour over the aubergine. Serve cold as a side dish. Popular all over the Middle East, this recipe becomes *baba ghanouj*, a delicious dip, when the ingredients are put through your liquidiser. Add lemon juice and coriander leaves for additional piquancy.

ENGLAND

Garlic was a 'pot-herb' in England until Elizabethan times when it fell out of favour. The diarist John Evelyn forbade its use in his salads.

Between January and October 1978, 1,549 metric tonnes of garlic were imported into England. Who is eating all the garlic? Not only the small percentage of Britons who were born or brought up in garlic-eating countries: English cooks have their own ways of introducing garlic into their dishes. Travelling abroad in greater numbers than ever before, they have brought home many new ideas; but some are their very own.

The Duckworth Duck

An exclusive recipe

Ingredients

1 British duckling, approx. 4½ lbs
salt
1 can (1 lb 12 oz) apricot halves
1 small onion, peeled and chopped
1 large clove garlic, peeled and crushed

2 tablespoons dripping and juices from roast duckling
2 level teaspoons plain flour
1–2 tablespoons dry French Vermouth

to serve: Watercress
Crispy garlic crumbs

Method

Preheat oven to moderate (350°F, 180°C, Gas Mark 4).

Pat the duckling dry inside and out with absorbent kitchen paper. Prick the skin all over with a fork and sprinkle with salt. Place the duckling on a grill rack in a shallow roasting tin, breast uppermost. Roast in a prepared oven, centre shelf, without basting for 2 hours then turn oven up to hot (400°f, 200°C, Gas Mark 6) and continue cooking for a further 15 minutes or until golden brown, crisp-skinned and cooked through. Meanwhile prepare the sauce and garnish.

Sauce: Drain the apricots, reserving the 8 firmest halves for garnish and arrange these on a small baking tin (use the syrup for a jelly or fruit salad). Purée the remaining apricots in a liquidiser or press through a sieve. Heat 2 tablespoons of dripping and juices from the roast duckling in a saucepan. Add the onion and garlic and cook, without browning, over very gentle heat until tender. Sprinkle in the flour and stir over heat 1 minute. Remove from heat and gradually blend in the prepared apricot purée. Return to heat and simmer 2 minutes, stirring throughout. Add French Vermouth and season well to taste. Heat the reserved apricots in the oven for the last 2–3 minutes of cooking time.

To serve: Arrange the well-drained duckling on a hot serving dish. Garnish with sprigs of watercress and the apricot halves filled with a few garlic crumbs. Serve the prepared apricot sauce and remaining crumbs separately.

Crispy Garlic Crumbs

Ingredients

2 tablespoons duckling dripping
1 clove garlic, peeled and crushed
6 heaped tablespoons fresh white
breadcrumbs
1 level tablespoon finely chopped parsley

Method

Heat the duckling dripping in a frying pan. Add the garlic and cook gently 1–2 minutes. Stir in the breadcrumbs until the dripping is completely absorbed. Continue frying, stirring as necessary until the crumbs are evenly browned and crisp. Stir in very dry finely chopped parsley.

Garlic and Fish Pie

Method

In a baking dish arrange pieces of cod fillet or cod steaks (about 1 lb for every three people). Sprinkle with chopped parsley. Cover with many thin slices of fresh garlic – at least 8 cloves for each pound of fish – and pour olive oil liberally on top. Season with lemon juice, sea salt and freshly ground pepper. Now slice newly boiled potatoes on top of the fish and garlic. Dot with pieces of butter, sprinkle with more salt and pepper, and bake at Gas Mark 5 (or 400°) until the potatoes are brown and the fish is cooked.

You may like to mince the garlic into the oil, or use the blender to make a garlic-and-oil mix. Do not hold back; this pie is sensational and the more garlic, the better.

Garlic Vinegar and Garlic Wine

Method

Put six peeled but uncut garlic cloves in a wide-necked bottle. Cover with wine vinegar or sherry. Cork the bottle securely. Shake it vigorously once a day for a week. Pour off the liquid and decant in small, well-capped bottles. A drop or two of the vinegar, or wine, will add distinctive flavouring to salad dressings, sauces and soups.

Garlic Sauce

Method

Put into a saucepan ten tablespoons of demi-glaze* and two tablespoons of tomato sauce. Bring to a boil and cook for a few minutes. Using a garlic press, add a clove of garlic and a dessertspoon of caster sugar. Serve this sauce with cold meats.

* Demi-glaze is a beautifully transparent brown sauce.

Garlic Oil

Method

Peel a large garlic clove and cut it into quarters. Drop the pieces into a bottle of good-quality vegetable oil and store in a cool pantry for at least a week. Useful for cooking, for salads and for marinades. Try brushing this oil over a chicken before roasting, or over roasting potatoes or on halves of tomatoes and mushrooms before grilling.

24

Park House Fennel, Artichoke and Garlic Soup

Ingredients

2 onions, cut into dice
2 cloves of garlic, chopped
6 bacon rinds
1 bay leaf
1 lb Jerusalem artichokes, peeled

1 lb fennel, trimmed and sliced
1½ pints chicken stock
1 cup thin cream
salt and black pepper

Method

Fry the onions, garlic and bacon rinds in a little oil. Add the bay leaf, the artichokes and the fennel. 'Sweat' the vegetables for a few minutes, then add the stock and seasoning and simmer until the vegetables are tender. Sieve the soup, or push through the fine blade of the *mouli*. Before serving, re-heat, then add the cream – or try evaporated milk, which works remarkably well.

Omelet Jane Stockwood

Method

Make a 2-egg omelet in the usual way and just before folding, slice very thinly one garlic clove and lay the slices evenly on top of the omelet in the pan. Fold over and serve immediately.

Chicken Imperial Sandieson

Ingredients

12 chicken drumsticks
(or enough chicken pieces for 6
  people)
1 packet grated parmesan cheese (4
  oz fresh)
1 cup breadcrumbs, home-made

  and lightly toasted
a fistful chopped parsley
2 cloves garlic, crushed
salt and pepper
about 4 oz butter

Method

Wash and dry the chicken pieces. Make a coating mixture from the cheese, breadcrumbs, parsley, garlic, salt and pepper. Melt the butter and dip the chicken pieces in it, then roll them in the coating mixture. Arrange them side by side on a buttered baking tin. Top each piece with a knob of butter. Bake in a 400°F oven (No. 5 or No. 6) for 1 hour, basting with pan juices after 30 minutes. Good hot or cold; what's left from tonight's dinner party can be tomorrow's picnic lunch.

Shoulder of Lamb with Spinach and Garlic Stuffing

Ingredients

A boned shoulder of lamb

½ lb packet of frozen spinach purée

½ lb lamb's liver

1 cup minced veal

1 egg

butter, salt and black pepper

2 cloves garlic

Method

Cook spinach and drain thoroughly. Fry liver in butter and then chop it up. Mix spinach, liver, raw veal, crushed garlic cloves, salt and freshly ground black pepper. Bind with beaten egg and stuff into cavity of shoulder. Carefully fasten with skewers and string. Spread joint with butter and bake about 1½ hours at No. 6 gas (425°F). Baste once or twice with pan juices. Remove skewers and string before serving. Stuffed joints always require longer cooking than plain roasts.

Health farms and health resorts are big business in England and the USA and are gaining in popularity in other countries. Champneys at Tring in Hertfordshire is one of the most famous and luxurious in England. Not surprisingly, the Chef uses garlic in his kitchen; and for calorie counters, he gives the number of calories per portion in his recipes. Neither is 'typically English' but both are adapted to the tastes of English dieters.

Tzanziki

serves 10   50 calories per portion
100 calories if you have two crispbreads

Ingredients

¼ cucumber, peeled

¼ cucumber, unpeeled and thinly sliced

2 cloves garlic, peeled

2 cups cottage cheese or curd

cheese

lemon juice

salt and pepper

2 sprigs fresh parsley

Method

Set aside the sliced cucumber and put the rest of the ingredients into your liquidiser. Blend until smooth. Pour into individual 'pot au crème' and chill. Garnish with sliced cucumber and serve with crispbreads.

Lamb Kebabs

serves 10   270 calories per portion without rice

Ingredients

2 lbs lean lamb, cubed	1¼ cups rice
10 shallots	a selection of finely diced
20 button mushrooms	vegetables, cooked separately
20 small tomatoes	and mixed together
oil for brushing	

Marinade

½ onion, cut into dice	½ pint yoghurt
garlic clove, crushed	bayleaf
lemon juice	

Method

Cut the lamb into 1 inch cubes. Put together the marinade in a shallow dish and marinate the lamb pieces for 24 hours, occasionally turning the meat. Skewer lamb with shallots, tomatoes and mushrooms. Brush with oil before broiling or grilling. Cook the rice and mix with the diced vegetables.

Mary Berry's Low Calorie Garlic Salad Dressing

Ingredients

1 teaspoon Dijon mustard	1 garlic clove
1 tablespoon wine or cider vinegar	salt and pepper to taste
1 tablespoon lemon juice	a sprinkling of artificial sweetener
1 small carton plain yoghurt	

Method

Tip the yoghurt into a screw-top jar. Crush the garlic and add it to the yoghurt with the other ingredients. Mix well and store in the refrigerator. A tablespoon of this dressing contains 10 calories.

Nineteenth Century Ways with Garlic

Garlic Gravy

'Cut a pound of lean beef into slices, and put them into a stew pan with two ounces of rasped ham, a scraped carrot, and one clove of garlic. Brown the meat slightly on both sides, then pour over it one pint of stock or water, a bundle of savoury herbs, another clove of garlic and a lemon sliced right through. Simmer gently for an hour, thicken the gravy with a dessert-spoonful of flour, mixed smoothly with a small quantity of water, and strain through a coarse sieve. Add salt and pepper to taste, and a little grated nutmeg.

'Sufficient for one pint of gravy.'

Garlic Paste

'Slice the cloves from 6 heads of garlic, and pound them in a mortar, moistening them occasionally with olive-oil until they form a smooth paste. Put the mixture into jars, cover with clarified butter, and keep in a cool place. This composition (commonly called agoli), is used for flavouring dishes with garlic. A little taken on the point of a knife will flavour a pint of gravy.'

Garlic Pickle

'Divide one pound of cloves of garlic, take off the skins, and lay them in a dish. Strew salt plentifully over them, and let them stand for two or three days. Wipe them and lay them in the sun to dry. Put one quart of vinegar into a preserving-pan, with a teaspoonful of salt, one ounce of whole pepper and one ounce of bruised mustard seed. Boil quickly, remove the scum, and throw in the garlic for three minutes only. Pour into a earthen jar, and, when cold, tie a bladder or four or five folds of paper tightly over the pickle. The vinegar must cover the garlic, and as it becomes absorbed, a little more may be added.'

Eggs and Garlic

'Pound ten cloves of garlic that have been boiled in water for twenty minutes – the water having been changed during the boiling – with a couple of anchovies; put them, when well pounded, into a stew pan, and add two tablespoonfuls of oil, the beaten yolks of two eggs, a tablespoonful of vinegar, some pepper and salt, and mix all together while being heated. Put the mixture on a dish, and serve with sliced hard boiled eggs. Four eggs will cut slices enough for this dish.'

Cassell's *Dictionary of Cookery*, 1877

Stokenchurch Pie

This was the pie farm-workers' wives made for them to take into the fields for mid-day dinner. The crust is made with hot water and the pie was served cold.

Ingredients

Pastry:
1 lb plain flour
½ lb pure lard
salt
hot water to mix

Filling:
1½ lbs any cooked meat
1 clove garlic
¼ lb macaroni
3 hard boiled eggs

Method

Make the pastry in the usual way and set aside while you prepare the filling. Mince meat and garlic together, moistening with a little pan-dripping or stock. Boil the macaroni and add to the meat. Cut eggs into quarters.

Roll the pastry into two circles and fit one carefully into a large pie tin. Put in half the meat mixture and arrange eggs on top. Cover with the rest of the meat and fit the pastry lid, cutting a hole for the steam to escape. Brush with milk and bake for at least half an hour in a hot oven.

FRANCE

France and garlic have a constant love affair – garlic is incorporated into *haute cuisine* and provincial cookery and is used in every region from the north to the south. Perhaps it is most strongly associated with Provençal cooking where it appears in its own right as a vegetable. Remember Garlic Purée: first oven-roast complete heads of garlic, then peel and purée them, seasoning with salt and fresh pepper and embellishing with a large, unpeeled garlic clove. Beautiful.

Croutons Frottés à l'Ail

Method

Rub each side of crisply fried triangles of bread lavishly with the cut side of a garlic clove and sprinkle with salt just before serving. These add zing to Bœuf Bourgignon, Coq au Vin or a purée of peas or haricots.

Emile Bernard's L'Aioli

Method

Take two garlic cloves per person, peel and crush completely in a mortar until it makes a paste. Gradually add a beaten egg yolk and a little salt. Pour in a trickle of olive oil, little by little, working the pestle round all the time. After having added the equivalent of ¾ cup of the oil, add the juice of a lemon and a little warm water, taking care that the mixture does not separate. If this does happen, empty the contents of the mortar into another bowl, put a second egg yolk and a little lemon juice into the mortar and very gently mix in the unsuccessful mixture. It is then ready to serve and will be a delicious, yellow, firm, oily, savoursome and gorgeous garlic mayonnaise.

Beurre aux Fines Herbes

Ingredients

3 egg yolks
2 gherkins, finely chopped
a few capers, finely chopped
1 garlic clove, chopped
parsley, chives, tarragon

4 anchovy fillets, chopped
½ cup butter
1 tablespoon tarragon vinegar
5 fl oz olive oil

Method

Blend these ingredients in a blender, or push through a sieve or *mouli*.
Pack into a china pot and allow to harden in the refrigerator.

Gascony Butter

Method

Thoroughly clean a good-sized bunch of fresh watercress, removing the
thicker stems. Wash, dry and mince finely. Rub a basin several times
with a freshly cut clove of garlic. Now work ¼ cup butter with a fork,
blend in the minced watercress and season to taste with white pepper
and salt.

These two butters are excellent accompaniments for grilled or baked
fish or pot-au-feu.

Tourain a l'Ail

Method

Peel a large handful of garlic cloves. Gently sauté them in groundnut oil
until just pale gold. Add water to the quantity of soup desired (about 3
pints), salt, half a bay leaf and a little fresh thyme. Simmer until the
garlic is really soft and then crush it with the back of a spoon against the
side of the pan. Beat 2 or 3 egg yolks in a bowl with a trickle of vinegar.
Just before serving, pour a ladle of the boiling soup on to the eggs,
mixing well. This mixture should then be poured back into the soup,
but do not boil it again.

A refinement is to simmer some shredded, deep-red skinned tomato
flesh in a little thin cream until barely cooked and add this to the soup
just before you add the egg mixture.

31

Aigo-Buido or Boiled Water Soup

Method

Put ten crushed cloves of garlic, a sprig of fresh sage, 2 tablespoons very finely chopped parsley, some coarse salt and a pinch of freshly ground pepper into a soup pot. Add 4 tablespoons olive oil. Pour in 10 cups of water and boil the soup for 8 to 10 minutes. Pour into a heated soup tureen and float on top of the soup a slice of bread covered with chopped parsley. This soup can also be served garnished with fresh eggs poached in the broth.

Spiced Velouté Soup

Method

Bring two pints of water to the boil in a saucepan. Add 6 heaped teaspoons of crushed garlic, $\frac{1}{3}$ powdered bay leaf, $\frac{1}{3}$ teaspoon powdered thyme, a pinch of powdered cloves, salt and pepper. Cook slowly for several minutes.

Now cut 20 small squares of thin white bread and bake in the oven until they are crisp and light brown. Place these croutons in a soup tureen and sprinkle them with a little olive oil and, if desired, some grated cheese. In another saucepan make a roux using a knob of butter and three tablespoons of flour. Add the spiced soup little by little to the roux and stir well to avoid lumping; let the mixture thicken. Beat a whole egg into a half-glass of white wine and add this to the soup, stirring constantly. When the whole is smoothly blended, pour the soup over the croutons and serve immediately.

Salade Niçoise

This is, perhaps, the most typical of all Provençal recipes. Quantities need not be exact; one ingredient may be increased at the expense of another. Basically, however, it is a mix of quartered lettuce, quartered firm tomatoes, quartered hard boiled eggs, tuna fish, anchovy fillets and black olives, tossed in a preparation of olive oil, tarragon vinegar, salt, pepper and a crushed garlic clove. Optional extras to the Niçoise may include cooked french beans, beetroot and artichoke hearts.

Ratatouille

Another traditional and very garlicky recipe from Provence and again quantities can be juggled round somewhat.

Brown 2 large chopped onions in olive oil. When they are slightly coloured, add 4 ripe tomatoes cut into quarters and 4 crushed garlic cloves. Cover the pan and simmer for 15 minutes. Next add 2 courgettes, sliced, 2 aubergines, peeled and cut into pieces and 2 large green pimientos, seeds removed and flesh chopped. Season with salt, pepper and nutmeg. Cover the pan and transfer to a slow oven for an hour. Good hot as a vegetable and very cold as an hors d'oeuvre.

Tossed Green Salad

Method

Whichever variety of lettuce you choose, it must be well washed, shaken in a salad basket and finally, each leaf dried individually. (The Swiss Zyliss salad dryer is an effective alternative.) Store salad greens in a polythene bag and keep in the refrigerator until needed.

Rub a wooden salad bowl with a cut clove of garlic. A subtle variation is to use the French 'chapon'. For this, cut up a garlic clove finely and cook it in butter. Add a large square of white bread (about 2 inches) and turn it in the pan until the bread is golden brown. Drain it on kitchen paper and place in the bottom of the salad bowl. Now add the lettuce, broken into pieces. This simple salad can be dressed with olive oil and lemon juice and seasoned with salt and pepper. Turn the leaves gently with wooden salad servers until each leaf glistens. Remove the 'chapon' before serving.

Garlic French Dressing

Ingredients

½ teaspoon dry mustard
salt, black pepper
caster sugar

2 tablespoons garlic vinegar
5 tablespoons olive oil

Method

Measure the dry ingredients into a screw-top container. (You will need less than a teaspoon of sugar.) Add the oil and vinegar and shake the bottle thoroughly. Pour the dressing over the salad and toss very gently before serving.

Another method: cut a clove of garlic in four pieces and put into the container with the rest of the ingredients. Allow to stand for at least an hour, then shake thoroughly. Remove the garlic pieces before serving.

Snails à la Narbonnaise

Ingredients

3 dozen snails, fresh or preserved (enough for 6 people)
½ pint dry white wine
3 tablespoons olive oil

3 cloves of garlic
3 egg yolks
1 oz almond powder
thyme, bay leaf

Method

If using fresh snails, they should have fasted for at least 2 weeks. Soak them in water for 1–2 hours with 2 handfuls salt, then wash several times in vinegar water. Plunge the snails into a stewing pan full of cold water and bring to the boil. Allow them to cool in the water. Draw them out of their shells with a sharp knife and cut their 'twists'. Heat the olive oil in a stewing pan, add the cloves of garlic but do not let them brown. Add the white wine and thyme and bay leaf (crumple one leaf) and season with salt and pepper. Cook for 10 minutes. Now remove the bay leaf and thyme and add the snails. Simmer for a few minutes, add the almond powder and keep warm on a corner of the stove.

Beat the yolks of eggs with a few drops of water and keep in a warm place. Add this mixture to the snails and remove from the heat. Do not let it boil.

Put 6 snails on each plate, share out the sauce, and keep the plates in a moderate oven for ten minutes before serving.

Cod à l'Occitane

Ingredients

1 lb salt cod
3 or 4 potatoes
2 eggs
1 lb tomatoes
about ½ cup margarine

3 cloves of garlic
salt and pepper
lemon juice/2 spoons
capers/2 oz black olives

Method

Soak the salt out of the cod for at least 12 hours, changing the water several times. Next day, boil the potatoes for 25–30 minutes until they are tender, and hard-boil the eggs. Bring the cod to boil in a fresh pot of water, adding a little salt. Cook gently for 5 minutes then remove the pot from the heat and let the cod cool in the water.

Cut the tomatoes in quarters and fry them in a little margarine. Add the garlic and seasonings. Now peel and cut the boiled potatoes in thick slices and cut the hard-boiled eggs into rings. Drain the cod and pick the flesh from the bones. Rub a baking tin with margarine and put in it, layer on layer, tomatoes, potatoes, cod, egg rounds, potatoes and tomatoes. Dot surface with margarine and put the baking tin into a very hot oven to 'burn' (really, to sear). Serve the cod dish very hot, having sprinkled the top with lemon juice and decorated with the olives and capers.

Perch à la Souveraine

Ingredients

6 perch	salt, peppercorns
½ bottle champagne	3 tablespoons oil
½ pint fish stock	4 tablespoons butter
2 cloves garlic	1½ tablespoons flour
bouquet garni, chives, basil	juice of 1 lemon

Method

Clean the fish, removing the gills and half the roe. Lay the fish in a fish-kettle and add the champagne, the fish stock, garlic, herbs and seasonings. Add the oil. Cook very gently on a low heat. When the fish is tender, remove from the liquor and strain it. Reduce it on a fast flame, then thicken with butter kneaded with flour, whisking the mixture constantly. Add the lemon juice. Before serving, skin the fish and arrange them on a hot serving dish, then coat with the sauce. You may like to reserve some of the chives for garnish.

This dish may be made with any fresh fish – trout, for example.

Braised York Ham à la Champenoise

Ingredients

1 9–11 lb ham	2 sticks of celery, cut into pieces
4 carrots, cut into pieces	2 bottles champagne brût
3 onions, stuck with 2 cloves each	light brown sugar
4 cloves garlic	potato flour
1 bouquet garni	

Soak the ham in cold water for 24 hours and then brush it to remove the white layer which will have formed on the rind. Place the ham in a roomy braising pan and cover entirely with cold water. Bring to the boil, then lower the heat and simmer gently so that the surface of the liquid barely trembles. Add all the vegetables and the bouquet garni. Allow 15–18 minutes to the pound of ham so that a nine-pound ham will cook for about 2½ hours. When the meat is tender, drain it and cut off the rind and some of the fat, but not too much. Pour the broth into another container and save it. Replace the ham in the braising pan and cover with the champagne and about 4 cups of the broth. Cover the pan and cook in the oven for another hour, basting frequently. Drain again, cover with a layer of brown sugar, and put into a hot oven to glaze and colour a nice brown. Reduce the stock by rapid boiling. Taste for seasoning and correct if necessary. Thicken the stock with a little potato flour mixed with some of the cold broth. Hand the sauce separately. Do not remove too much of the fat from it.

Roast Chicken Stuffed with Garlic

Method

You will need a fresh (not frozen) bird for this dish. Make sure it is at room temperature before you begin. Prepare the chicken for roasting in the usual way, washing and drying inside and out and rubbing the cavity and skin with salt. Now peel *several heads of garlic* until you have enough to almost completely fill the cavity in the bird. Add a good lump of butter and loosely truss. Rub the bird with melted butter and set on a rack in a roasting pan. Roast the bird very, very slowly, basting several times with pan juices and melted butter. When the garlic is creamy (you will have to test it) sprinkle the bird with a little herb – thyme or tarragon – and raise the oven temperature to brown the skin. The creamy garlic cloves inside are bliss! and even better, this recipe with its lavish use of garlic never fails to win over the doubtful. The French garnish this dish with sprigs of fresh watercress. If you are lucky enough to have any of the meat left over, it is superb with salad next day, quite unlike the rather boring cold chicken we are sometimes obliged to serve, and eat. Don't waste the carcase or the skin; they make a terrific base for soup, impregnated as they are with garlic.

Daube Provençale

Method

Rub 2 lbs of rolled ribs of beef with salt and pepper. Brown the meat evenly in a little hot oil in a cast-iron casserole. Add several thick rashers of bacon, cut into small pieces, 3 cloves of garlic, 4 large ripe tomatoes, peeled and cut into quarters, and a sprig of thyme. Pour over 4 tablespoons of brandy and cover the casserole securely. Cook in a very slow oven – Regulo 2 – (325°F) for 2¼ hours. Add 4 cups button mushrooms and cook a further 15 minutes. Remove the beef, slice it, and lay on a bed of pasta, moistening with the gravy and garnishing with finely chopped parsley and garlic.

Calf's Ribs à la Languedocienne

Ingredients

4 calf's ribs	4 oz green olives
4 oz raw ham	a little goose dripping or butter
1 tablespoon minced onion	salt, pepper
1 clove garlic	

Method

Fry the calf's ribs in the fat or butter and when they are well browned, add the onion, the raw ham cut into little dice, the garlic and salt and pepper. Cover the pan closely and allow to simmer for about half an hour. Stone and scald the green olives, drain them and add to the pan for the final 5 minutes of cooking. To serve, arrange the ribs on a hot dish, decorate with the olives and pour over them the warmed-up pan juices.

Languedoc Cassoulet Toulousain

This ambitious dish originated in the Toulouse-Carcassone area and has achieved world-wide popularity.

Ingredients

1¾ pts haricot beans	specialist delicatessens)
1 lb pork brisket	1½ lbs mutton brisket
¼ lb goose preserve (available in	1 polony – about 9 oz

37

9 oz small sausages
1 knuckle of pork
½ lb pork rind
3 tablespoons tomato juice
½ lb onions

2 carrots
6 cloves garlic
2 cloves
breadcrumbs, salt and pepper

Method

Soak the haricot beans in water overnight. Next day, drain them, discarding the water, and put them in a stewing pan with the carrots, onions pricked with the cloves, 3 cloves of garlic, the pork brisket, the knuckle of pork and the rind. Cover with water and bring to the boil, skimming carefully. Simmer. In another pan, place the mutton brisket cut into pieces, some lard and salt and pepper. Brown the meat, add one onion chopped and 3 cloves of garlic. Add the tomato juice. Cover the pan, adding a little of the water from the haricot beans from time to time.

When the beans are almost tender, remove the carrots, onions and garlic cloves. When the mutton is almost tender, add it to the beans with the polony, the goose preserve and the sausages. (Prick the sausage skins first.) Let the whole simmer for half an hour. Next, take all the meat from the beans. Cut up the sausages, the goose preserve, the pork brisket and the polony – removing the skin – in slices or in pieces. Cut the rind in square pieces.

Take a large oval dish and arrange the ingredients as follows: first a layer of haricot beans, then the pieces of mutton and goose, then another layer of beans, then the pork brisket, the rind, polony and sausages. Sprinkle liberally with breadcrumbs, dot with goose dripping. Brown the whole lightly in the oven and serve very hot.

Hare à la Champenoise

Ingredients

1 4½ lb hare
salt and pepper
2 tablespoons Armagnac
8 thin strips pork fat
3 onions
6 shallots

6 cloves garlic, finely chopped
bouquet garni
6 peppercorns
1 glass dry white wine
butter and flour
watercress

Method

Skin and gut the hare, trimming carefully. Season with salt and pepper. Sprinkle the Armagnac inside and then put back the liver, kidney and lungs. Wrap the hare in half the slices of salt pork and truss. Line the bottom of a braising pan with the rest of the pork fat and heat it. Place the hare in the pan, add the onions cut in two, the chopped shallots, the garlic cloves, crushed, and the bouquet garni. Add the peppercorns and the white wine, cover the pan, and cook over a very gentle heat for about 1 hour. When the meat is tender, remove from the pan and set aside while you make the sauce. Make a roux with butter and white flour, adding the strained liquid from the pan. Cut the hare into pieces and arrange them on a platter. Decorate with watercress. Hand the sauce separately.

Moules à la Bordelaise

Ingredients

1 quart mussels
2 bay leaves
sprig of mace
2 oz butter

2 oz flour
4 tomatoes, peeled and chopped
2 cloves garlic
fresh parsley

Method

Wash mussels carefully in several waters, brushing well and removing 'beards' with a sharp knife. Shells should be tightly shut. Tap with the knife and discard those which remain open. Cook mussels in tightly lidded pan with the bay leaves, mace and $\frac{1}{2}$ pt of water (or half water, half wine). When the shells are open, remove mussels and strain pan liquor. Now make a roux with the flour and butter, allowing it to brown lightly. Add the tomatoes, 1 garlic clove, parsley and seasonings and thin with the strained pan liquor. Cook gently, adding the mussels in time to heat them through. Serve sprinkled with *persillade* (parsley and second garlic clove minced together).

GREECE

Greece, and its rich network of islands, uses garlic in many of its famous national dishes. The character of Greek garlic is quite distinctive, as those who have visited Greece, or enjoyed Greek foods in other countries, can testify. The cuisine travels well: but there are some dishes one rarely meets away from the country. One is their *Bakaliaros Skordalia*, a deep-fried salt cod served with garlic sauce. The sauce is made from garlic, softened white bread, ground almonds and egg yolks, sharpened with fresh lemon juice. It is, in fact, not very different from a garlic sauce popular in medieval England, for it was customary then to mix garlic and ground almonds with bread crumbs.

Taramasalata

Ingredients

6 slices white bread	juice of 1 lemon
6 oz smoked cod's roe	1 tablespoon finely chopped
a small onion, finely chopped	parsley
2 cloves garlic, crushed	green olives
½ cup olive oil	triangles of hot toast

Method

Trim the crusts from the white bread and soak the slices in water, then squeeze them until they are thoroughly drained. Put the bread, cod's roe, onion and garlic into an electric blender and blend at slow speed, adding the olive oil and lemon juice alternately in small amounts until the mixture reaches the consistency of a smooth paste. Turn into a serving bowl, sprinkle with the finely chopped parsley and garnish with green olives. Serve the taramasalata cold with triangles of hot toast, or more rustically, with hot pitta bread.

Rice with Tomatoes (Bourani)

Ingredients

1½ cups rice	2 lbs tomatoes, peeled
5 cloves garlic	¼ cup olive oil
1 tablespoon salt	some chopped parsley
3 tablespoons sugar	

Method

Wash and drain the rice well. Cut the tomatoes into slices and discard the seeds. Put tomatoes into a saucepan with the garlic, salt, sugar and olive oil. Cook this mixture for about 10 minutes, then add the parsley. Add 2 cups of water, and bring to the boil. Add the rice, stir once and cover the pan. Cook over medium heat, without stirring, until the rice has absorbed all the liquid, about 15 minutes. Serve cold.

Roast Lamb à la Greka

Ingredients

a 4 lb leg of lamb	juice of 1 large lemon
5–6 cloves of garlic	1 cup hot water
salt and pepper	2½ lbs medium-size potatoes
¼ cup butter	

Method

Wash and dry the meat and place in a roasting tin. Cut the garlic into slivers and insert them into incisions made in the lamb. Season the meat with salt and pepper. Peel and quarter the potatoes and arrange them around the meat in the roasting pan. Sprinkle meat and potatoes with the lemon juice. Add the hot water and bake in a moderate oven for about 2 hours. When the lamb is done, remove it to a hot platter. If the potatoes are not brown enough, place them under the grill for a few minutes.

HUNGARY

Land-locked Hungary grows and exports garlic – the region best known for both onion and garlic growing is the south-eastern town of Makó, border country. Although some of the famous Hungarian stews, like *gulyas*, would be incomplete without garlic (and there is a dish called *Paloc*, made with mutton and potatoes, caraway seeds and red paprika in which it is a very necessary ingredient), for the most part the Hungarians use garlic subtly.

Mutton 'Gulyas Soup'

Ingredients

4½ lbs mutton	salt
¾ cup fat	4 potatoes
1 large onion	2 green peppers
1 clove garlic	3 tomatoes
1 teaspoon caraway seeds	½ pt white wine
1 tablespoon paprika	

Method

Cut the meat into cubes and sauté them in fat in a deep saucepan, stirring well. Add the onion, finely chopped, the garlic, caraway seeds and paprika. When the meat has lost its red colour, add enough boiling water to cover it. Simmer until the meat is nearly tender, then add the potatoes, peeled and cut into cubes, the peppers, deseeded and cut into strips, and the tomatoes, peeled and cut into quarters. Now add about a pint of boiling water. Cook the soup until the meat is done, adding the wine just before serving. This soup is enough like a stew to serve as a main course.

Lamb Soup from Szerged

Ingredients

2 lbs lamb from the leg or shoulder cut into cubes	2 lbs lamb bones
	¾ lb mixed vegetables (try carrots,

42

parsnips, turnips)
½ cup fat
1 large onion
paprika, salt, ground pepper
2 cloves garlic

6 oz streaky bacon
4 oz mushrooms
parsley sprigs
½ pt red wine
pasta

Method

Place bones and vegetables in a heavy pan, cover with cold water, bring to the boil and skim carefully. Now fry the meat with the garlic and onion in the fat, add the paprika and other seasonings and stir well. Cover the pan tightly and allow to cook very slowly until the meat is tender, adding a little wine from time to time. Now fry the bacon which has been cut into dice and add the pieces to the meat pan. In the fat left from the bacon, fry the garlic and mushrooms and the finely chopped parsley. Add these to the meat as well. When the meat is tender, add the vegetables and stock from the bones. This soup can be served with any suitable pasta. Dish out the pasta first into generous soup bowls, then ladle the soup over it.

Savoy Cabbage Casserole

Ingredients

about 4 lbs Savoy cabbage
6 eggs, separated
salt and pepper
½ pt sour cream
¼ lb bacon
1 large onion

1½ cups rice
2 cloves garlic
1¼ lb minced pork
1 cup breadcrumbs
1 cup grated cheese

Method

Cut the cabbage into largish squares and boil in salted water until half cooked. Strain and set aside. Meanwhile parboil the rice in water, adding some of the fat. Set aside. Now mix the egg yolks with the seasonings, then fold in the stiffly beaten whites and the sour cream. Add the pieces of cabbage to this mixture. In a pan, fry the bacon which has been cut into pieces, lift them from the fat and fry the onion, garlic and pork in the same fat. Now add the rice to this mixture.

Grease an oven dish of a suitable size and dust it well with breadcrumbs. Arrange a layer of the meat mixture, then a layer of the vegetables and eggs, repeating the process until the dish is full. Dot the top with the remaining fat, strew thickly with breadcrumbs and grated cheese, and bake in a moderate oven until bubbling hot (about 20–25 minutes). A good dish for a buffet supper.

Debrecen Pork Chops

Ingredients

2 lbs boned loin of pork
1 Hungarian 'Gyulai' sausage, the
  same length as the loin
1 bottle Riesling wine
1 tablespoon lard

1 green paprika (a pepper)
1 tomato
1 onion
2 cloves garlic
salt, pepper

Method

Make a hole through the centre of the joint, horizontally, and insert the sausage. Rub the meat with salt and pepper and brown it in the hot lard. Add the wine and vegetables, cover, and braise slowly, adding water if necessary to prevent burning. When the meat is tender, drain and slice very thinly. The sausage in the middle looks attractive and has a fine flavour. Strain the gravy and pour over slices of meat. This is a spectacular dinner party dish.

Stewed Pork in Sauerkraut

This dish resembles the previous one in that pork and 'cabbage' are principal ingredients. But note the differences as well.

Ingredients

6 oz bacon
¼ cup fat
1 onion
2 cloves garlic
3½ lbs lean pork cut into cubes
salt, pepper, marjoram
¼ cup flour

½ lb pasta
4 eggs
4 tablespoons butter, softened
1 cup sour cream
1 lb sauerkraut leaves
½ bottle white wine

Method

Cut the bacon into small cubes, fry them and remove from the pan. Add more fat and in it fry the onion and garlic. Add the pork and seasonings, sprinkle with flour and add enough water to make a sauce. Now add the pieces of bacon and the vegetables, cover the pan and allow the stew to cook slowly.

Meanwhile, cook the pasta in salted water and drain it. In a separate bowl, mix the butter and egg yolks, the sour cream and the cooked pasta. Add the meat mixture and fold in the beaten egg whites. Line an oven dish with the sauerkraut leaves and turn the meat and pasta mixture into it. Pour over the wine and cover with any sauerkraut leaves remaining. Bake in a moderate oven for 30 minutes. When the dish is finished, allow to cool slightly then turn out and cut into squares. Serve with additional sour cream.

Veal Paprika

Ingredients

1–1½ lbs stewing veal, cubed
1 oz lard or butter and lard mixed
4 onions, sliced in rings
2 garlic cloves, roughly chopped
1 tablespoon paprika
1 tablespoon flour

½ pt stock or water
3 tablespoons tomato purée
salt and pepper
1 carton plain yoghurt or soured cream

Method

Brown the meat in hot fat and set aside. Fry onion rings and garlic in the same fat and sprinkle with paprika and flour. Lower the heat and add stock, tomato purée and seasonings. Add the meat and cook very gently for an hour. Stir in yoghurt or cream just before serving. Delicious with broad egg noodles seasoned with crushed garlic and fresh parsley.

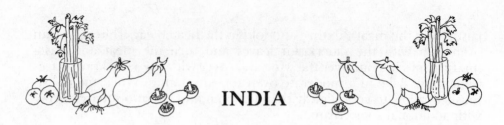

INDIA

Some Indian cooks are lavish in their use of garlic, and others, as Savitri Chowdhary points out in his book on Indian cooking, never touch either onions or garlic.

The style of cooking ranges from the strongly flavoured to the bland. One typical vegetarian dish calls for the making of a garlic and ginger sauce, with crushed coriander seeds, fennel seeds and onion. Green beans are cooked in the sauce, drained, seasoned with butter and lemon juice, and served very hot.

This sauce can be used more than once. Cool it quickly and refrigerate it, bringing it to a full boil before adding another batch of beans.

Saag Bhajee

Method

Put about 4 tablespoonsful of vegetable oil in a pan with 2–3 cloves of peeled garlic. Fry until the garlic turns a light brown, turning it in the oil. Add some chopped onion – about a handful – stir, then add some Haldi powder (available from Indian grocers) and a very small amount of curry powder. Stir again. Now add the leaves of fresh spinach, perhaps ¼ lb, and cook in the oil and spices for about 5 minutes until the leaves are wilted and covered with the sauce. Serve at once.

Prawn Patia

Method

Put 1 cup of peeled prawns per person in a pan with vegetable oil and fry for two minutes. Add 2–3 garlic cloves and cook until the cloves are golden brown. Now add chopped onions, green peppers and tomatoes, and a selection of Indian spices. Stir several times and leave for 4–5 minutes on a low heat. Serve with rice or chapattis.

Kofta Curry

Ingredients

2 lbs raw lamb, minced
1 onion, chopped finely
ground ginger
ground turmeric
2 garlic cloves, pressed
salt
2 eggs
for the gravy:

½ onion, chopped
1 garlic clove
1 tablespoon olive oil
chili powder
turmeric
coriander
ground cumin seed
½ cup water

Method

Mix the meat with the rest of the ingredients and form into balls or rissole shapes. Bake these in the oven until they are brown. Make a gravy, browning the onion and garlic in the olive oil and adding the remaining ingredients. When it is hot, pour over the meat balls.

Tarka Dall with Garlic

Method

Cook ½ lb of lentils in sufficient water to cover, adding salt, a few bay leaves, and a stick of cinnamon. When the lentils are soft, remove from the heat and allow to cool. In a pan, melt a tablespoon of butter and add a sprinkling of mild spices. Add the lentil mixture, heat, and put into a dish in the oven to keep hot. Now put 3 tablespoons of oil in a pan with 3 garlic cloves cut into slivers, a few onion rings and some cumin seeds. Fry until the onion and garlic are brown. Pour on top of the dall and serve. Tarka Dall is a traditional side dish. Indian spices come in several strengths; ask at a specialist shop for the ones you prefer.

ISRAEL

Jews from many countries have settled in Israel, so Israeli cookery reflects the cuisines of a dozen homelands, with a Middle Eastern flavour all its own. The land of milk and honey rejoices in an abundance of fresh fruits and vegetables – and grows garlic as well. We have included a vegetable dish and a meat dish and one dish which features tomatoes.

Broad Bean Salad

Ingredients

1 tin broad beans (or use frozen, fresh or left-over beans)
1 clove garlic
1 small carton plain yoghurt
squeeze of lemon juice
oil
salt
parsley and dill

Method

Drain the beans and place in bowl. Peel and press a clove of garlic over the beans. Make a dressing of yoghurt, lemon juice, oil and salt, and fold this into the beans. Top with chopped parsley and dill. Very quick and particularly delicious.

Sweet and Sour Meat Balls

Ingredients

1 lb chopped round steak
¼ cup brown rice, uncooked
1 clove of garlic, chopped
1 grated onion
½ teaspoon sea salt
freshly ground pepper
1 egg or ½ cup tomato juice
chopped parsley
1 tablespoon bread crumbs

a little fat for frying
for the sauce:
1 cup tomato juice or tomato soup
1 cup diced celery
1 green pepper, diced
3 tablespoons light brown sugar
4 tablespoons cider or wine vinegar

48

Mix all the ingredients for the meat balls in a bowl – use either egg or tomato juice to bind the mixture, then form it into balls about the size of a walnut. Set them in a cool place while you make the sauce. Combine all the ingredients for the sauce in a pan, cover and allow to simmer. Now slowly fry the meat balls in a little fat, turning them so they brown evenly. Pour off the excess fat and add the sauce. Cover the pan and cook the meat balls for 20 minutes, then uncover and cook another few minutes. If necessary, thicken the sauce with a little cornflour mixed with cold water. Serve with broad egg noodles, or cooked spaghetti.

Spicy Tomatoes

Ingredients

6 tomatoes
¼ cup parsley, finely choped
2 cloves garlic, pressed
1 teaspoon onion, finely chopped
¼ teaspoon salt

¼ teaspoon black pepper
1 teaspoon lemon juice
¼ teaspoon spicy mustard
4 tablespoons olive oil

Method

Cut the tomatoes in half. Mix together the parsley, garlic, onion, salt, pepper, lemon juice and mustard and spread this mixture over the tomato halves. Heat the oil in a frying pan and put in the tomatoes, spread side up. Cook them gently until they are hot through, then transfer to a shallow baking dish and continue cooking for 15 minutes in a hot oven (400°F or Gas Mark 6). Serve hot or cold.

ITALY

Italy is not only an enormous vineyard from top to toe and heel but it also produces large amounts of onions, leeks and garlic. The yearly garlic crop averages nearly 7,500 metric tonnes. In 1977 the value of the crop exported was £480,998. The area which produces most is Campagna, and only 8 per cent of its crop is exported. Sicily produces nearly 1,000 metric tonnes a year, again for local consumption, while the Veneto region on the mainland managed to grow nearly 900 tonnes. Here, 60 per cent of the crop is exported.

The relationship between Italy and garlic is so intimate that we have decided to describe in some detail how each region of Italy makes use of garlic in its indigenous dishes; the variety is staggering:

Piedmont: *Camoscio in salmi* – chamois meat cooked in a garlic sauce.

Lombardy: *Tinca carpionata* – an assortment of fishes, marinated before being fried; the marinade includes garlic cloves.

Trentino: *Lepre alla trentino* – hare, jugged in a stew of olive oil, garlic, onion, white wine and seasonings. A very spicy dish.

Venetia: *Baccala alla vicentina* – dried cod cooked in milk and flavoured with onions, garlic, anchovies, cinnamon and seasonings.

Liguria: *Cima alla genovese* – beef stuffed with sweetbreads, lard, chopped pork, fresh peas and garlic and onion.

Emilia-Romagna: *Risotto alle vongole* – the rice is cooked in a sauce of oil, tomatoes and parsley, and clams and garlic are added to it.

Tuscany: *Zuppa di datteri alla viareggina*: this soup is made from a variety of mussel which are called 'dates' because of their shape. Garlic, olive oil, tomatoes, pepper and salt are cooked together, and the mussels are added.

The Marches: *Porchetta* – a whole sucking pig, stuffed with rosemary, garlic and pepper, either roasted in the oven or over embers on an open fire.

Umbria: *Spaghetti ad aglio ed olio* – a popular, quick-to-make dish. The spaghetti is tossed in olive oil which has been heated with garlic and ginger.

Latium: *Abbachio* – an unweaned lamb (which has never eaten grass) is roasted in the oven *alla cacciatora*, that is, with a dressing of olive oil, vinegar, rosemary, garlic and, sometimes, anchovies.

The Abruzzi e Molise: *Polpi in Purgatorio* – cuttle fish cooked in oil; tomato, parsley, garlic and lots of pepper are used to season it, and the resulting sauce is both rich and hot (hence, Purgatory).

Campania: *Zuppa alla marinara* – a delicious stew made with several varieties of fish, garlic, pepper, salt, parsley and tomatoes, and served with slices of fried and toasted bread.

Apulia: *Cozze Gratinate* – a dish to be enjoyed *al Taranto*; the mussels, one shell removed from each, are covered in olive oil, parsley, garlic and breadcrumbs and then browned in the oven.

Calabria: *Melanzane Farcite* – Aubergines stuffed with tomato, garlic, anchovies, seasoned with oil, parsley and black pepper.

Sicily: *Anelletti Gratinati* – Little 'rings' of cuttle fish, dipped first in oil then in breadcrumbs, salt, pepper, parsley and garlic and then baked on trays in the oven.

Bagna Cauda

This Piedmontese speciality packs a punch thanks to its many cloves of garlic and fillets of anchovy. A good dip for raw vegetables.

Ingredients

½ cup butter
½ cup olive oil
8 cloves of garlic, sliced very thinly

16 anchovy fillets, finely chopped
freshly ground pepper

Method

Heat the fats together in a small skillet. Cook the garlic and anchovies briefly and grind in the pepper, letting all the ingredients steep together over a very low flame. Keep the mixture warm for dipping.

Oil, Garlic and Anchovy Sauce

Ingredients

6 tablespoons olive oil   6 anchovy fillets
1 clove of garlic, slightly crushed

Method

Heat the oil and garlic together, but do not allow the oil to boil. Mash the anchovies with a sharp fork until they form a paste, then add to the oil, stirring well. Serve as a sauce for *al dente* spaghetti.

Crostini

This Italian version of garlic bread makes the buttery version we know appear very delicate.

Method

Take some crusty white bread, baguette size and shape, and cut into slices about half an inch thick. Now toast or grill the bread and quickly rub with garlic, as much as you like, on both sides. Pour the finest dark green virgin olive oil over the toast (again, according to your taste), sprinkle with salt and eat. If the toast has cooled during this operation, place in a hot oven to reheat.

Marcello Turco's Recipe for Spaghetti Aglio e Olio

The advice of the cautious – 'use sparingly, don't overdo' – is thrown to the winds here with spectacular results.

Ingredients

1½ lbs spaghetti   huge bunch parsley, chopped
many cloves of garlic – at least 8   wine glassful olive oil
small red pepper or chili (the kind   salt and pepper
   that burns if you bite it)   tumbler of white wine

Method

Cook the spaghetti *al dente*. In a saucepan, heat the oil and add the garlic, red pepper, parsley, salt and pepper and the wine. Cook for a few minutes then add the spaghetti, mixing well.

Drunken Pork

Method

Sprinkle a dozen pork chops with salt and pepper and fry them over a moderate flame with two cloves chopped garlic, a good handful of chopped parsley and a good pinch of fennel seed. When the chops are golden brown, pour over ½ bottle of Chianti Classico, cover the pan and cook until the chops are tender. Remove the chops to a serving dish and keep them warm while you reduce the 'gravy'. Pour it over the chops and serve very hot. Excellent with floury potatoes or pasta.

Pizza

for the base:
½ oz dried yeast
1 teaspoon brown sugar
2 eggs beaten with a little milk
8 oz wholewheat flour
1 oz fat
1 teaspoon salt

for the sauce:
1 onion, chopped
1 tablespoon oil
2 cloves garlic, crushed
15 oz tin Italian tomatoes
2 teaspoons tomato purée
salt, pepper, mixed herbs

for the top:
8 oz grated mature cheddar cheese, a dozen black olives, tin of anchovies and a selection of garnishes: fried bacon bits, cut up ham, flaked tuna fish, thinly sliced salami, green pepper pieces, slivered mushrooms.

Method

Cream yeast and sugar together, mix in eggs and set aside for 10 minutes. Sieve flour, add salt and work in fat. Add yeast mixture to flour, mix well and leave in a covered bowl for 40 minutes. Gently fry onion and garlic in oil. Drain off most of the liquid from tomatoes and add them with the purée. Mix well and simmer for 10 minutes. Add seasoning and herbs.

To assemble, flatten dough and fit into dish measuring at least 10 inches. Spread sauce and cheese on top and arrange olives and anchovies from centre outward in starfish shape. Decorate with some of suggested garnishes. Bake in moderate oven for 35–45 minutes.

KOREA

Korean cookery has been influenced by the Chinese and Japanese. It is usually highly seasoned and heavily spiced. Meal preparation can take a long time, for it is the custom to offer up to twelve dishes to one's guests. We have given one charmingly named dish; but the Koreans also serve simpler dishes which can be adapted to Western kitchens very easily. Try their mixture of rice and bean sprouts. First warm a little sesame seed oil in a pan, add minced garlic, chopped spring onions, top and bulb, and then 1 cup blanched bean sprouts and cooked rice – you can vary the amount according to your taste. Fold in about a tablespoon of sesame seeds and quickly heat the vegetables. Season with a little soya sauce.

A Magic Recipe from Korea

Method

Best beef, entrecote or fillet, is recommended, but rump or rib will do. Cut beef into thin slices. Make a mixture of soya sauce, white sugar, a great deal of crushed garlic (5 cloves) and marinate the beef in this for three or four hours. The saltiness of the soya becomes overbearing if four hours is exceeded. Remove the meat from marinade and wipe it dry. Cook the meat, for preference, on a barbecue, or a ridged cast-iron steak pan heated on the stove. The cooking time is very short: twenty seconds a side.

Serve with absolutely plain rice, and a sauce composed of soya sauce, garlic, and a small amount of vinegar.

N.B. Be prepared: Korean garlic is the strongest of all.

MEXICO

In her book on the cuisine of Mexico, Diana Kennedy recommends frying onion and garlic gently, without browning, until soft. The Mexicans call this 'acitronar'. She also describes how garlic is 'toasted' on a hot comal or skillet. You let the cloves cook through on both sides for a few minutes, then peel away the charred skin from the softened flesh.

Mexico is one of the world's major producers of garlic. The cuisine resembles the Spanish, but there are significant differences. Maize, or corn, was originally cultivated during the Mayan civilisation. We have included one recipe combining it with another of Mexico's indigenous plants, the chili.

Mexico has an abundance of fish; there is a wonderful soup made from white fish, tomatoes, mushrooms and fresh peas, seasoned with garlic, onions and fresh herbs, with olives and croutons and a pinch of cinnamon for flavouring. For another fish dish, lay a whole fresh haddock (about 2½ pounds) in a baking dish, add thin slices of garlic, salt, pepper and lemon juice, and cover with sliced onions and tomatoes, 3 tablespoons of olive oil and some thinly sliced lemon. Bake, covered, for about half an hour at Gas mark 4, 350°F, occasionally basting with the pan juices. Uncover and bake another 10 or 15 minutes, basting once or twice. Sprinkle with chopped parsley. Very Mexican.

Guacamole

Method
Select 2 very ripe avocado pears. Mash the pulp to a smooth paste in a bowl that has been rubbed round with a cut clove of garlic. Add 2 teaspoons lemon juice, 4 teaspoons grated onion, 1 teaspoon salt, ½ teaspoon chili powder, mixing well with a silver fork. Taste, increasing the amounts of salt and chili powder according to your palate. To prevent guacamole from darkening, cover with a very thin layer of mayonnaise, and mix this in just before serving. This is an ideal dip for raw cauliflower florets, radishes and carrot strips.

Aguacate (Avocado)

Ingredients

3 ripe avocados
1 clove garlic, finely chopped

1 cup olive oil
½ cup cider or wine vinegar

Method

Peel and slice the fruit. Blend the oil and vinegar with the garlic and pour it over the avocados. Cover and allow to soak overnight. To serve, drain the avocado and arrange the slices on lettuce or chicory leaves.

Season with a *sharp French dressing*:

Ingredients

the oil and vinegar/garlic mixture
   used to marinate the avocados (8
   tablespoons)

½ teaspoon salt
¼ teaspoon paprika

Method

Shake the ingredients in a small jar.

Corn off the Cob with Green Chili and Garlic

Ingredients

about 5 ears of corn
2–4 green chilis
1 clove of garlic, cut fine

3 tablespoons lard or olive oil
scant teaspoon salt
freshly ground pepper

Method

Cut the corn from the cobs. Heat the fat in a frying pan and add the corn, chilis and garlic. Cover tightly and cook very slowly until the corn is tender, 10–15 minutes. Add the seasoning. If the corn seems dry, add several tablespoons of boiling water while cooking. You can use tinned corn, very well drained, for this recipe – the cooking time will be much shorter.

Kidney Bean Soup

Ingredients

1 lb frijoles (red kidney beans)
2 quarts cold water
1 onion, sliced
1½ tablespoons salt

2 cloves garlic
1 chili, red or green, pulped
   or 1½ teaspoons chili powder
1 tablespoon oregano

Method

Pick the frijoles carefully and then soak overnight in cold water. In the morning, drain the beans and cover with fresh water. Boil them slowly for 4–6 hours, all day if possible. When they are half done, add the salt. You may also need to add more water. When the beans are tender, add the onion, garlic, oregano, chili, and boil until the vegetables are soft. Rub through a *mouli* or sieve and reheat, adding boiling water until the soup is of the consistency of a purée. Serve with small cubes of bread deep fried in fat.

Chili Sauce

Ingredients

1 small onion, chopped	1 cup chili pulp (made from fresh chilis)
1 clove garlic, chopped	
2 tablespoons fat	or 4–6 tablespoons chili powder mixed with 1 tablespoon flour
½ teaspoon salt	
pinch oregano	(an egg)

Method

Fry the onion and garlic in the fat until they are tender, add the salt and oregano. Blend in the chili pulp or the chili powder and flour. Add enough water to make a thin gravy and boil for about 20 minutes. If a milder sauce is wanted, add a beaten egg just before removing from the fire; or use more flour and less chili powder.

Chili is meant to protect against colds, aid the digestion, clarify the blood, and develop robustness and an ability to resist the elements. A rival to garlic?

Pollo con Arroz

Ingredients

1 chicken – 3½ to 4 lbs	1 clove garlic, chopped
½ tablespoon salt	1 cup uncooked rice
3 tablespoons fat	pinch saffron powder
1 onion, chopped	

Method

Cut the chicken into 8 pieces. Cover with boiling water and boil for 15 minutes, skimming from time to time. Add the salt. In a separate pan, heat the fat, add the onion and garlic and stir in the rice. Cook together until the ingredients are well mixed but not browned. When the chicken is nearly tender, add it and the broth to the rice and simmer until the rice is done. Add saffron power just before serving.

Chili con Carne

Ingredients

½ cup flour
salt and pepper
1 lb beef, cut in cubes
3 garlic cloves
½ onion, sliced

2 tablespoons lard
2 tablespoons chili powder
½ cup hot water
1 teaspoon oregano

Method

Put ½ cup flour in a strong paper bag with seasonings. Add the meat and shake well. Now fry garlic cloves and onion in lard until they are light brown, remove them and fry the meat. Make a paste of chili powder and water and pour over the meat. Sprinkle with oregano and cover pan tightly. Simmer until meat is very tender.

NEW ZEALAND

New Zealand is well known for its lamb and much New Zealand lamb has travelled to England since the first hazardous journey in the 'Dunedin'. The quality is excellent, especially suitable for garlic flavouring.

Spiced Leg of Lamb

Ingredients

1 leg of New Zealand lamb
1 tablespoon sugar
1 teaspoon dried mustard
1 teaspoon ground cloves
1 teaspoon ground ginger

1 tablespoon lemon juice
salt/pepper
1 clove garlic
parsley sprigs

Method

Insert the garlic, cut in slivers, into the skin of the leg, marking each point with a small sprig of parsley. Now mix the rest of the ingredients and spread over the lamb. Roast at 350°, Gas Mark 4, for 30 minutes per pound. In New Zealand, they remove the parsley and garlic before serving.

Whole Baked Pumpkin with Garlic

Digby Law's excellent *Vegetable Cookbook* (Auckland, 1978) recommends slicing the top from the pumpkin, removing seeds and soft pulp, and putting in butter, salt, pepper and 2 or 3 sliced garlic cloves. Bake an hour at medium heat and serve whole, slicing like a cake. Try this with vegetable marrow (overgrown courgettes), slicing lengthwise.

 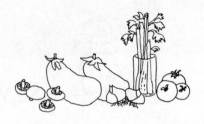

PERU

Peruvian cooking is strong, exciting and colourful. Both onions and garlic are widely cultivated and there is an apocryphal story that a Peruvian garlic grower sent his son to an English public school on the profits of his garlicky half acre. Ajos (garlic) and aji (chili) form the backbone of this country's cuisine with its African, Spanish and Indian influences.

'Cebiche' of Octopus

Ingredients

1 octopus	2 medium sized onions
4 large cloves of garlic	5 spring onions
4 limes	2 Seville (bitter) oranges
1 teaspoon chili powder	1 fresh chili
salt and pepper	

Method

Beat the octopus with a stick all over. Then wash it, cut it in small pieces and cook it in salt water. When it is tender, drain it well. While still hot, add it to the following mixture: combine diced onions, crushed garlic, chili powder, fresh chili cut small, the juice of the limes and the oranges, and salt and pepper to taste. Marinate octopus in this mixture for two hours. If it is not sufficiently 'sharp', add the juice from 1 or 2 more limes.

Serve with corn on the cob and sweet potatoes (yucca). All 'cebiche' dishes are served cold, but the vegetables can be hot.

N.B. In London, octopus is obtainable most of the year from R. Rowe & Son, Harrow Road. It is imported from Spain.

Arroz con Pato (Duck with Rice)

Ingredients

1 plump duck	8 cloves of crushed garlic
salt and pepper	2 teaspoons yellow chili powder

1 cup chopped coriander
lard
1 large onion, chopped small
2 tomatoes, chopped

3 whole fresh chilis – seeded, and
cut into large slices
½ lb spring peas
4 cups rice

Method

Clean the duck and cut into pieces. Melt lard in a large saucepan, add salt, pepper, garlic, chili powder, tomatoes and, finally, the duck. When half cooked, add the coriander and uncooked peas. Continue cooking slowly until the duck is almost ready. Then add the uncooked rice and the fresh chilis. Stir and cover. Cook until rice is tender and then serve.

When adding the rice, make sure there is not too much liquid or the rice will be soggy.

Aguadito

Ingredients

6 pieces chicken, boned
large onion, finely chopped
2 large garlic cloves, chopped
3 tomatoes, peeled and chopped
1½ cups fresh coriander leaves
2 cups long grain rice

2 cups lager
6 cups water
1 cup cooked green peas
1 red pepper, sliced
oil
salt to taste

Method

Fry chicken until brown but not cooked. Remove from pan, then fry onion and garlic until both are light brown. Add tomatoes, coriander which has been chopped or liquidised with a little oil and water, and chicken pieces. Mix well and add water and lager and bring to boil. Stir in rice, lower heat and cook, covered, for 20 minutes. Add peas and red pepper. This is a green 'soup'. When rice is tender and meat cooked, liquid rises to the top and chicken sinks to the bottom. Serve at once or rice will absorb all the liquid.

In Lima, rice is always cooked with garlic. It is fried in a little oil, then water is added, then the rice is boiled in the usual way.

From the Commercial Office of the Peruvian Embassy in London

SOVIET UNION

Garlic is grown in almost all regions of the Soviet Union where the climate is considered suitable, but most production is concentrated in the North Caucasus, the Southern Ukraine, the Crimea and in Kazakhstan and Uzbekistan.

Ukrainian Borshtch

There are dozens of ways of making borshtch; here is one of the simplest.

Ingredients

1½ lbs meat, preferably brisket of beef
10 young beetroots
2 oz pork fat
juice of half a lemon
1 slice streaky bacon, cut into pieces
5 tablespoons tomato paste
1 bay leaf
1 carrot, chopped
a small bunch parsley, stems and tops chopped
1 onion, chopped
half a white cabbage, cut into pieces
2 potatoes, peeled and cut into pieces
1 green pepper deseeded and cut into strips
5 garlic cloves
salt, pepper, a little sugar
sour cream

Method

First cook the brisket in water to cover until it is tender, skimming occasionally. Remove the meat from the broth. Chop 5 of the beetroots roughly and sauté in the pork fat in a soup pan with half the lemon juice, the bacon and the tomato paste. Cover with some broth from the brisket, add the bay leaf, and simmer for about half an hour, until the beetroots are tender. Now grate the remaining beetroots on a coarse grater into another pan, pour a little of the broth on them, add the rest of the lemon juice and cook until these beetroots are tender, about fifteen minutes. Strain this liquid, discarding the grated beetroots. In a separate saucepan, cook the carrot, the chopped parsley and the onion in a little butter and add to the soup pan. Add the cabbage, potatoes and green pepper, then the beetroot water and the garlic cloves. Simmer until all the vegetables are done. Cut the brisket into pieces and add to the borshtch. Season the soup with salt, black pepper and a little sugar. Bring the borshtch to the boil, cover the soup pan and let the soup stand for half an hour. When you are ready to serve, put a generous dollop of the sour cream into each bowl, ladle meat and vegetables on top, and fill the bowl with soup. Borshtch is delicious cooked one day and served the next.

Cabbage with Nuts and Garlic

Ingredients

a medium-sized cabbage
2 onions, chopped finely
5 garlic cloves, pressed

a wine glass of walnuts, ground
herbs: thyme, basil, tarragon
salt and pepper

Method

Cut the cabbage into cubes and boil in salted water. Drain and arrange on a dish in a thin layer and put a weight over it. In an hour, drain the juice from it carefully and mix the cabbage with the walnuts, garlic, onions, herbs, ground black pepper and a little salt. Make this several hours before required, as the flavours improve with keeping. Serve cold as a starter, or as a side salad.

Kirghiz Langman

Ingredients

2 lbs boneless lamb
lard
3 onions
3 tablespoons tomato paste
$\frac{3}{4}$ lb sliced radishes
$\frac{1}{2}$ lb green pepper

black pepper and salt to taste
2 cloves garlic, crushed
stock
parsley, dill
vinegar
fine cooked noodles

Method

Cut the lamb into strips. Fry in the lard with the onions, radishes, green pepper, salt and pepper, and garlic, turning over and over until the meat loses its colour and begins to brown. Now add the tomato paste, cover the pan, and allow the contents to simmer for 15 minutes. Pour in a little stock and continue cooking for another 20 minutes. Arrange the noodles on a hot platter and pour the meat on top. Garnish with chopped parsley or dill. Serve with vinegar as a 'sauce'.

Steamed Meat Balls with Garlic

Ingredients

1 lb finely minced meat
¼ lb cooked rice
a pinch of salt

2 garlic cloves, minced
butter

Method

Mix meat, rice, garlic and salt very thoroughly together, pounding well. Shape into three or four balls and steam them until they are cooked through – about half an hour. Serve with fresh butter.

Quenelles of Pike or Perch

Ingredients

fish
¼ lb cooked rice
2 cloves garlic

2 oz melted butter
salt and pepper

Method

For this recipe, the rice should be cooked until it is glutinous, then cooled. Scale, skin and wash the fish. Mince with the rice and crushed garlic. Add the butter and seasonings. Knead well with hands until the mixture is smooth. Form into 10–12 quenelles and steam. Serve with more butter.

SOUTH AFRICA

The strongest influences on the cuisine of South Africa come from the early settlers – Dutch, English and French Huguenots. There are also dishes typical of Malaya and parts of India, and some Arab influences as well. Garlic has been cultivated in South Africa to satisfy all these ethnic groups; but it is still a conservative country and while a few dishes like *Sassaties* (grilled marinaded mutton) and certain chutneys call for the inclusion of garlic, many of the curries and stews do not include it.

Casserole Steak Constantine

Ingredients

2 lbs lean beefsteak
good pinch mixed herbs
2 cloves garlic
pinch nutmeg
salt and pepper
a little dripping

4 oz bacon, cut into pieces
$\frac{1}{4}$ pint dry red wine (or very dry sherry)
1 lb small onions
1 tablespoon plain flour
2 cups mushrooms

Method

Cut the beefsteak into serving pieces and brown in a little fat. Arrange in an oven-proof casserole, seasoning with salt and pepper, herbs and nutmeg. Brown the bacon pieces in the same pan with the whole onions and garlic and set aside. Now pour off most of the fat from the pan and make a roux with the flour, adding the red wine and stirring until the mixture is smooth. Add the bacon and vegetables. Pour this sauce over the meat. Cover the casserole and bake at 350° (Gas Mark 3) for 1½ hours. Half an hour before serving, add the mushrooms. Skim off surplus fat before serving.

 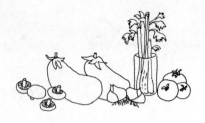

SPAIN

Much of the garlic imported into Great Britain comes from Spain, although France is the largest consumer of Spanish garlic within the Common Market. Every year brings a dramatic increase in the amount of garlic Britons consume, so that the 282 tons purchased from Spain in 1977 may soon seem a very small amount indeed. 97 per cent of Spanish garlic is purple-skinned, but some white garlic is also grown.

Garlic Olives

Ingredients

1 jar of green olives, pimiento-stuffed
1 cup of pitted black olves
1 cup olive oil
4 cloves of garlic, crushed
3 tablespoons wine vinegar

Method

Drain the green olives and combine with the black olives in a screw-top jar. Add the crushed garlic cloves to the olive oil and vinegar and pour over the olives. Shake well. Store the jar in the refrigerator at least 24 hours before serving. Another method: cut the garlic cloves into narrow strips and stuff a piece into each pitted black olive. Pack both kinds of the olives into a jar and top up with olive oil and a tablespoon of the wine vinegar. Store as above. Keep the marinade for next time.

Garlic Sauce

Ingredients

1 medium potato, cooked and peeled
2 cloves garlic, crushed
1 cup olive oil
2 tablespoons wine vinegar
½ teaspoon salt
dash pepper

Method

Mash potato; stir in crushed garlic. Gradually beat in olive oil, then stir in vinegar, salt and pepper.

This sauce is especially good with lamb, but also delicious with hot vegetables – broccoli, green beans, etc.

'Allioli' (garlic and oil)

Ingredients

6 garlic cloves   fine table salt
fine olive oil

Method
Peel the garlic cloves, put them in a mortar and mash with pestle. Now add fine salt and oil (from an oil pourer so that it can be added drop by drop); keep turning the pestle in one direction. The quantity of oil depends on the volume desired.

This sauce thickens like a mayonnaise and can be used for salads or fish dishes.

Gazpacho

This is the famous cold soup of Andalusia.

Ingredients

1 large clove garlic, crushed   chopped, or 1 20 oz tin of
2 slices white bread, cut into cubes   tomatoes
½ cup water   ¼ cup grated onion
¼ cup olive oil   2 cups ice water
1 teaspoon salt   2 tablespoons wine vinegar
2 lbs ripe tomatoes, peeled and

Method
Combine the garlic, bread, water, olive oil and salt and let the mixture stand several hours or overnight. Add the tomatoes; beat in blender or mixer until pureed. Add the grated onions. Chill until ready to serve, then add the ice water and vinegar. Top with an assortment of garnishes; these are almost as important as the soup, creating colour and crunch.

Garnishes
1. Saute small cubes of white bread in olive oil until crisp and golden brown.
2. Peel a cucumber, remove the seeds and dice the flesh. Sprinkle with salt.

3. Hardboil 3 eggs, chill them well and chop fine.
4. Remove the seeds from a green pepper and cut into small dice.

Quick Gazpacho

Ingredients

2 lbs soft tomatoes	1 cup olive oil
1 cucumber	⅓ cup vinegar
1 small green pepper	½ cup mayonnaise
1 small onion	salt and pepper
1 tablespoon paprika	croutons for garnish
1 large slice white bread	

Method

First set aside a few slices of tomato and cucumber for the garnish. Put the rest of the ingredients through the mincer and then the blender. Chill thoroughly. Garnish with the tomato and cucumber slices, and the croutons.

Sopa Mallorquina

Ingredients

4 tablespoons olive oil	strips
6 cloves garlic, minced	3 pints of water
2 medium sized Spanish onions, chopped	heart of a small cabbage, chopped
2 florets of cauliflower	3 tablespoons chopped parsley
2 tomatoes, roughly chopped	1 bay leaf, broken into small pieces
1 small red and 1 small green pepper, deseeded and cut into	several slices of stale bread
	1 to 2 glasses dry white wine
	salt and pepper

Method

Warm the oil in a heavy saucepan, add the garlic, onions and the cauliflower. Cook these vegetables very slowly for about 10 minutes until they have softened but not browned. Add the tomatoes and peppers and simmer for 15 minutes. Heat the water and add it slowly to the other ingredients and bring the whole to the boil. Now add the cabbage, parsley and bay leaf. Season to taste. Cover the saucepan and simmer for about 2 hours. Break the bread into small pieces and add them to the soup – continue cooking until the bread is soft but not mushy. Before serving, add the white wine. Any of the following vegetables may be substituted for the tomatoes: green beans; peas; asparagus; artichokes or mushrooms. Serve the soup very hot.

Costelles de Vedella Amb All

Ingredients

8 veal chops	lard
3 cloves garlic	chopped parsley
salt	breadcrumbs

Method

Cut the chops into neat rounds with a sharp knife. Fry them in a pan until they are brown. Remove from the pan and rub the meat well with fine salt and then with the lard. Mix the parsley, chopped garlic and breadcrumbs together and spread the mixture thickly over the chops. Grill for 15 minutes. Once the crumb mixture is slightly brown, the chops will be tender. Serve with potatoes fried in fat.

Escallops de Ternera

Ingredients

6 veal escallops, each weighing about 4 oz	2 cloves garlic
3 tablespoons olive oil	2 tomatoes, peeled and sliced
1 tablespoon lard	1 cup roasted hazelnuts, ground
2 medium sized onions, thinly sliced	1 small glass white wine
	some chopped parsley
	salt and pepper

Method

Fry the veal in a skillet with the olive oil and lard for about 5 minutes on each side. Remove the meat and keep it hot. Now fry the onions and garlic in the same oil, add the tomatoes and season with salt and pepper. Next stir in the ground hazelnuts until the mixture forms a paste. Thin this with the white wine and add the parsley. Pour the sauce over the escallops and serve very hot.

Paella

There are almost as many recipes for Paella as there are villages in Spain. This one makes an attractive and savoury party dish.

Ingredients

1 4-lb chicken cut into small pieces
1 teaspoon saffron (use tumeric if saffron is not available)
4–5 cloves of garlic
olive oil
2–3 onions, chopped
1 green pepper, deseeded and chopped
¼ to ½ lb Chorizo sausage, finely chopped
4–5 slices unsmoked streaky bacon, cut into dice
½ to ¼ lb cheap white fish – coley for example
¼ to 1 lb squid, if available
4 oz peeled prawns
1 pint mussels if in season – clean and steam in the usual way
12 oz rice
1 dozen unpeeled prawns
1 small tin red peppers
2 lemons cut into quarters

Method

Remove the skin from the pieces of chicken and use it to make a strong stock. Season it with salt and pepper and add the saffron. Keep the stock hot. In the paella pan, or a very large shallow frying pan, fry the pieces of chicken with the garlic cloves in olive oil until they are evenly browned. Remove the meat and garlic and fry the onions and green pepper in the same oil, adding more if necessary. Add the sausage, bacon, fish and squid, turning them in the oil; now add the rice and mix lightly until all these ingredients are well coated with the oil. Measure out four times as much stock as there is rice, using a teacup for measuring, and add it to the pan. The stock must be hot. Return the chicken to the pan and let the food cook very slowly on top of the stove (not in the oven). It will take about 20 minutes for the rice to absorb the liquid. Add the peeled prawns after 15 minutes. Turn off the heat and decorate the pan with the mussels, the unpeeled prawns and the red peppers cut into strips. Serve with lemon quarters.

SWITZERLAND

Surrounded by France, Italy and Germany, and influenced by their cooking, Switzerland has managed to develop one or two typically Swiss dishes – the Fondue, for one, but there are others. There are also excellent, and elaborate, patés which are days in the making – garlic is included in these dishes, and in the creation of certain savoury sausages.

Fondue Neuchâteloise

Method

Rub two cloves of garlic around a *caqueron* (that is, an ovenware dish with a handle which will take the heat of top-of-the-stove) and then chop the garlic cloves very small and scatter them over the base of the dish. In it place 1 lb 2 oz of grated Gruyere cheese which has been blended with about ½ cup of cream cheese. Add a pint of white Rhine or Riesling wine, diluted if it is very strong with a little water, and a pinch of white pepper. Mix well and bring slowly to the boil, stirring carefully with a fork. Next, in a small wine-glass of kirsch mix 1½ teaspoons of potato flour (*fécule*) until it is smooth enough to stir into the fondue.

Keep the fondue hot in a chafing dish and serve with a bowl of bread (preferably French) or rolls cut into half- or three-quarter-inch cubes. Everyone spikes a piece of bread with a special three-pronged fondue fork and dips it into the bowl. Delicious with a chilled white wine.

THAILAND

Thailand has a delicate, almost dainty cuisine, yet Thai food is not lightly perfumed by garlic but heavily permeated with it. The result: an unusual array of foods, not to everyone's taste, but with distinctive characteristics. A sparkling example of much garlic leading to subtle flavouring.

N.B. Brown sugar can be used in these recipes instead of palm sugar, although of course the flavour will not be the same. *Nampla* (a fish sauce) should not be too difficult to find; soy sauce with anchovy essence added to it can be used as a not entirely satisfactory substitute. Coriander leaf and root are both available in specialty shops, but a little crushed coriander seed will, again, suffice.

Nam Prik

(A typical Thailand sauce served with raw and roasted vegetables – a highly specialised taste)

Ingredients

1 teaspoon salt	shredded young mango
dry salted shrimps	*nampla*
10 cloves garlic, finely chopped	palm sugar
5 tablespoons kapi (a paste made from salted shrimp, available in specialty food shops)	chili
	lime juice

Method

Pound together salt and shrimp until they are fine. Mix in the other ingredients.

Boiled Eggs, Thailand Style

Method

Pound together some coriander, garlic and peppercorns. Stir over heat for a few minutes in a little lard. Add cubes of pork cut from the loin with the skin on. Cover with water, season with *nampla* and palm sugar. Bring to a boil, skim. Add the shelled, hardboiled eggs and cover the pan tightly. Cook until the pork is tender.

Some people cook the pork first, in one piece, then cut it into cubes.

Yam of Roses

'Yam' is pronounced 'yum' and means 'salad'.

Ingredients

1 breast of chicken
1 lb of lean pork
¼ lb of prawns or crayfish
about 4 tablespoons of hard pork fat
7 shallots
10 cloves of garlic, chopped finely

nampla, sugar and lime juice
about 3 tablespoons of coarsely ground roasted peanuts
the petals of 10 roses
3 sprigs of coriander
3 red chilis, shredded

Method

Boil the meats, drain and cut them into small pieces. Mince the shallots and fry with the chopped garlic in hot fat until brown – do not burn. Lift from the fat and set aside to cool. In a bowl, blend together the seasonings, add the pieces of meat, the peanuts and the rose petals. Add half the shallot and garlic mixture and arrange the meat on a platter. Sprinkle with the rest of the shallots and garlic, the leaves from the coriander sprigs and the shredded chilis.

Yam of Beef

Ingredients

1 lb beef
3 sprigs coriander
10 cloves of garlic
sugar

nampla
chilis – about 4 small ones, crushed
lime juice
2 finely shredded onions

Method

Roast the beef – it should be rather underdone. When it is cold, slice as thinly as possible and lay the slices on the dish you will serve it from. Pick the coriander leaves from the stalks and soak them in cold water. Crush

73

the garlic and add the sugar, *nampla*, crushed chilis and the lime juice. Pour the mixture over the beef and top with shredded onion and coriander leaves.

This dish may be made from left-over rare roast beef.

Fried Cabbage

Cooked the Thai way

Ingredients

10 cloves of garlic	sugar
about ½ cup pork cut from the loin into small pieces	pepper
¼ cup prawns or crayfish	about 3 cups of young green cabbage, chopped
nampla	

Method

Crush the garlic cloves, or mince them very finely, and brown them in hot lard, being careful not to let them burn. Add the pieces of pork; cook and stir until they are done. Add the prawns and seasonings, and last of all, the cabbage. For a crispy finish, the heat should be strong and the cooking rapid. Use a wooden spoon to keep the food in motion.

Pigeon in Sweet and Pungent Mixture

A Thai side dish

Ingredients

1 pigeon	1 tablespoon vinegar
1 cucumber	a sprinkling of sugar
1 onion	2 tablespoons soy sauce
2 tomatoes	1 clove garlic, finely minced
2 green peppers, deseeded	chopped coriander leaves
1 tablespoon flour	freshly ground pepper

Method

Remove the meat from the bones of the bird and cut into pieces. Slice all the vegetables except the garlic, cutting the green peppers into small diamond shapes. Blend the flour, vinegar, sugar and soy sauce together. Fry the garlic in a little oil until it is light brown. Add the meat pieces and stir for a few minutes. Then add the rest of the vegetables and the blended liquid. Stir well. When the meat is cooked, arrange the mixture on a plate with the chopped coriander leaves and the freshly ground pepper on top.

Mā Ho (Galloping Horses)

A side dish

Ingredients

1 lb pork, lean and fat mixed
5 cloves garlic
3 tablespoons lard
4 tablespoons roasted peanuts, coarsely ground

nampla
salt and pepper
oranges
coriander leaves
chilis

Method

Chop the pork into very small pieces. Crush garlic and fry in the lard until light brown. Add pork, peanuts and seasonings. Peel the oranges and separate into their natural sections, then cut each section open at the back. Fill each piece of fruit with the pork mixture, and decorate with coriander leaves and chilis.

Pork Boiled with Garlic and Bamboo Shoots

Ingredients

1 lb bamboo shoots
1 lb pork, cut from the loin
10 garlic cloves

pepper, coriander root, *nampla*, palm sugar
stock

Method

Plunge bamboo shoots into boiling salted water and cook until bitter taste is gone and vegetable is a pale yellow colour. Drain and set aside.

Cut the pork into pieces about 1½ inches square and cook them in a saucepan until the fat runs. Pound together garlic and seasonings and add to the meat. Stir until the meat is covered with the seasonings, then add the bamboo shoots and the stock to cover. Cook until the meat is tender.

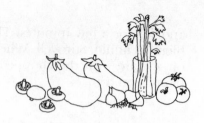

USA

Garlic has gained in popularity in USA since the end of World War II. America has always been a melting pot of cuisines, but the use of garlic was once confined to ethnic groups or was an integral part of the regional cuisines of south, southwest and west (e.g., Chili con carne with its Mexican influence). Not surprisingly, therefore, garlic is cultivated in Louisiana, Texas and California.

Since the nineteen forties America has adopted more sophisticated attitudes, and garlic is now widely used.

Caesar Salad

This is *the* classic American salad for garlic lovers.

Ingredients

1 large romaine lettuce	1 egg
4 slices white bread cut into small dice (trim off the crusts)	squeeze of lemon
	6 anchovy fillets
garlic-flavoured olive oil (about 6 fl oz)	salt and pepper
	2 oz parmesan cheese
1 garlic clove	

Method

Wash and trim the lettuce, break the leaves into small pieces and set aside. There should be no moisture on the leaves. Sauté the diced white bread in garlic-flavoured olive oil, about 2 oz, until the cubes are golden brown. Drain them on kitchen paper and set aside. Now rub the inside of a large wooden salad bowl with a cut garlic clove. Toss in the lettuce and season it with salt and pepper. Very gently toss the lettuce with 4 oz of garlic olive oil until each piece glistens. Now boil the egg for 1 minute and break it into the salad, again tossing the lettuce very gently. Add the lemon juice and the anchovy fillets which you have finely chopped. Again, toss very gently. Just before serving, add the grated cheese and the croutons and toss lightly again.

Serve with hot French bread.

76

Aubergine Lee

Here is one of the ways Americans use garlic powder. As this is an American recipe, it should be called 'Eggplant Lee'. Aubergine prepared this way makes a delicious vegetable dish, or you could serve each person with two slices as a starter.

Method

Peel enough aubergine to allow two or three slices per person. Cut the slices half an inch thick and spread one side with half the soft butter mixture.* Arrange the slices on a baking sheet with the butter side down – you will probably need two sheets – then spread the top sides with the rest of the butter mixture. Bake in a pre-heated 400° oven (gas mark 5) for ten minutes, turn the slices and bake another ten minutes. Sprinkle with finely chopped parsley and chives. Garnish with lemon slices.

* soft butter: to sufficiently softened butter add grated onion and its juice, a teaspoon of finely chopped parsley, salt, pepper, tarragon, garlic powder, sweet basil and chives. Mix well until easy to spread.

Kenneth Durant's Garlic Lamb Chops

Method

In a saucer put roughly chopped garlic cloves and sea salt, at least one clove for each chop. Using a sharp fork, mash garlic and salt together until the mixture is almost a paste. Grill lamb chops on one side, turn, lavishly cover uncooked side with garlic mixture and grill until chops are done.

Pâté George Beiers of Cape Cod

Ingredients

1¼ cup chopped onion
2 finely minced cloves of garlic
1 lb pork, medium ground
1 lb veal, medium ground
½ tablespoon freshly ground black pepper
1 tablespoon salt

¼ teaspoon mace
½ teaspoon allspice
½ lb fresh pork fat, finely diced and browned
3 eggs
4 fl oz Madeira, reduced to 2 oz/
3 fl oz cognac

1 lb chicken, duck or pheasant
meat, cut into strips about ½
inch wide, but as long as
possible

20–25 pistachio nuts
a few sliced truffles
1¼ lb sliced bacon, blanched and
the slices dried

Method

First fry the onion until golden, and add the finely minced garlic. Set aside. In a bowl, combine the pork and veal, add the garlic and onions, the seasonings, the pork fat, the eggs, the cognac and the Madeira. Line either one large or two small pans with ⅔ of the bacon slices. Spoon over them a third of the meat mixture and arrange half the pieces of poultry on top. Spoon in another third of the meat mixture and arrange sliced truffles and pistachio nuts on this layer. Cover with the remainder of the sliced bacon. Cover the pans carefully with aluminium foil. Bake the paté in a larger baking tin with an inch of boiling water in it, in a pre-heated 350° oven (Gas mark 3) for 1½ hours (slightly less if you are using two pans). Remove from the oven, cool, then chill with weights on top.

Black Bean Soup

Ingredients

1 lb black beans
salt and pepper
2 stalks celery, chopped
1 medium onion, chopped
2 cloves garlic, chopped

2 teaspoons cornflour
juice of ½ lemon
½ lemon cut into very thin slices
2 hard-boiled eggs, sliced
a little parsley, very finely chopped

Method

Soak the beans overnight in water to cover. In the morning, drain the beans and cover again with water and bring slowly to the boil, skimming until the water is clear. Add salt and pepper. Cook celery, onion and garlic in a little oil in a covered pan and add to the soup. Cover the pan and cook slowly for a very long time until the beans are tender. Sieve the soup or push through a medium blade *mouli* – it should not be too smooth. Mix the cornflour with a little water and stir into the soup, bringing again to the boil. Add the lemon juice just before pouring the soup into a heated tureen. Put 1 slice of lemon and two slices of egg on top of each bowl of soup as you serve it. Garnish with the parsley.

Bachelor's One-Dish Supper for Two

Ingredients

2–4 chops, lamb or pork
½ tin tomatoes
1 green pepper, deseeded and sliced in rings
1 onion, sliced in rings
½ cup long grain rice
3 garlic cloves
a little stock
salt and pepper
chopped parsley

Method

Salt a heavy skillet and when it is hot, sear the chops on both sides. Remove to a casserole or baking dish. Distribute the green pepper and onion rings between and around the chops. Now tip the tomatoes into the skillet and slice and add the garlic cloves. Swirl the tomatoes and garlic around the skillet until they are bubbling hot, and scrape into the casserole. The rice should now be added – be sure it is covered with liquid; if there doesn't seem to be enough, add a little beef stock. Add salt and pepper, and cover the casserole with a tight fitting lid. Bake in oven at medium heat; or cook on top of the stove at a low heat, for about 45 minutes. Sprinkle the parsley on top of the chops and serve with garlic bread and a salad – and wine. This dish can be made in an infinite variety of ways: try it with four chicken pieces, or with veal chops, or even fish – but if you use fish, don't add it until the rice is nearly cooked.

Fresh Kielbasa

A Polish Garlic Sausage From the USA

Twenty men (and 5 women whose sole task is to peel the garlic) meet in the kitchens of St Mark's Orthodox Church in Bethesda, Maryland, every year to prepare 400 pounds of this sausage for the Church's annual Christmas Bazaar. The recipe comes from Mr John Cibulsky of Endicott, New York, whose sister, Helen Gonsa, is in charge of the food preparations for the Bazaar.

Ingredients

3½ pounds pork butt, coarsely ground (if pork is very fatty, trim away some of the excess fat)
1½ pounds boneless shoulder of veal, coarsely ground
1 small whole head of garlic

1 tablespoon salt   6½ tablespoons water
1 tablespoon coarsely ground fresh   1 pound sausage casings
  pepper

Method

Blend the garlic with the water in a blender. Mix it with all the remaining ingredients by hand. Take a small amount of meat mixture and form into a patty. Fry it and taste it for seasoning. Let meat mixture stand overnight in the refrigerator to blend flavours.

Prepare casings by washing thoroughly, fitting the casings over the tap in the sink and filling slowly with water. Repeat several times and then store casings in cold water in the refrigerator until ready to use. Stuff the sausages by holding the casing over the end of the meat grinder and slowly grinding the meat mixture. Work the mixture down until it fills the casing. When the sausage is completed it should be about 1½ inches in diameter and 12 inches long. Tie off and then tie the two ends together in a circle. Repeat for the rest of the sausage meat. To cook: Fill a shallow baking pan with ⅛ inch water and add one of the sausages. Place in 375° oven and bake for 45 minutes or until slightly golden in colour. Turn the sausage over carefully (being careful not to prick the casing) and reduce oven heat to 350° and bake an additional 20 minutes.

(One pound of casings will be too many for this quantity of meat mixture but you can pack the remaining casings in salt and store in your refrigerator or freezer.)

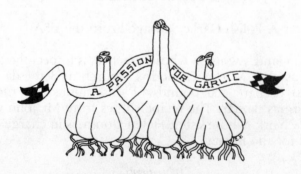

Garlic and Wine

There are plenty of wines, of all colours, which hold their own with garlic, and most garlic-laden dishes are more delicious when accompanied by wine. The countries and regions which produce garlic and garlic-focused food often produce complementary wines.

With so many wines to choose from, are there any useful rules when you are serving dishes which feature garlic? Here are the views of the Wine Development Board:

About the only wines which wouldn't, normally, go with garlic-based dishes, are those light white wines which are particularly subtle and delicate, and thus more likely to be overpowered. There would also be a clash if the wines were anything sweeter than medium dry. All this assumes that, even when garlic figures quite generally in the cooking, the actual amount used each time is relatively sparing. For dishes which specifically require strong garlic, one would be better off with pretty full-bodied wines, e.g., Côtes du Rhone, the heavier Burgundies, or, among whites, a crisp Muscadet, Pouilly Fuissé, Alsace Riesling, Johannisberger or Frascati Secco. On the other hand, how do you equate this with the fact that the garlic-laden dishes of the south like aioli or Salade Niçoise are usually eaten with the lighter wines (including rosés) of Provence and Languedoc? Alors ... back to square one.

So the field is splendidly open. The following selection will give you a wide choice. We have chosen these wines because they 'work' with garlic. You can omit the 'heavier Burgundies' – they are expensive, and we have listed plenty of reasonable alternatives. Middle-priced and cheap wines are good with garlic dishes – and if you choose a very cheap or generic red, try the following tip from the last cellarmaster at the Café Royal: Put one drop of tepid water into the decanter and the decanted red wine will show every hidden merit. But don't fall for that invidious monster 'cooking wine' – a wine for cooking must always be drinkable. Remember too that the alcohol in wine vanishes in cooking; only the flavour remains.

Here is a primer of wine-buying. There are many other wines and many other sources to buy from, but here you can begin your voyage of discovery:

ARGENTINA Wines from Argentina are considered a luxury in neighbouring countries like Peru because import duties are high, but in England Argentinian wines are good value. They are naturally good with all garlic dishes. Try *Primado Savya Red* (Victoria Wine) and *Franchette*, red and dry white. The latter comes in 1½ litre bottles (Harrods, etc.).

BULGARIA *Red Sofiya* (Justerini & Brooks Ltd.).

CHILE *Cabernet Rerservado*, red (J. & B. Ltd.).

CORSICA and SARDINIA *Domaine de Torraccia, vin de Corse, Porto Vecchio*, is pale in colour but very fully flavoured. The quality of Corsican wines has been much improved in recent years. This wine is obtainable through Lay & Wheeler Ltd., Colchester. *Domaine de Furgoli, A.C. Ticzano*, can be found at Christopher's, London. *I Piani* (Sella e Mosca) is a dry cherry red wine from Sardinia, obtainable at Tanners of Shrewsbury, while *Canonau Rosso* (Sella e Mosca) can be bought at Avery's of Bristol among other outlets.

ENGLAND Every English vineyard produces a highly individual wine – not always true even in France. Wine production flourished in England from Roman settlement days until Henry VIII dissolved the monasteries. Now there are hundreds of acres under viniculture and not even Henry could halt their progress. Most English wines are white, a few are poor and thin, several have more than sufficient character to complement garlic. *Adgestone*, Kenneth Barlow's famous Isle of Wight wine, is not unlike a Loire white. *Kelsale*, from Suffolk, is also a fine choice (both available from Adnams of Southwold). *Chilsdown*, Singleton near Chichester in West Sussex, produce a remarkable wine with the power of a *Pouilly Fuissé* (Tanners of Shrewsbury), and Sir Guy Salisbury-Jones has achieved the impossible: made Hambledon more famous for its wine than as the birthplace of cricket. *Hambledon* is a wine with a great deal of body and deserves its fame. (It is widely available.) *Merrydown Apple Wine* is made at Horam, East Sussex and qualifies as a 'country wine'. By EEC law, wine should be made from the juice or 'must' of grapes; but this dry apple wine goes well with most garlic dishes, especially those featuring pork.

FRANCE Many of the world's greatest vineyards are in France. From Alsace, try a *Gewürztraminer Reserve* (Ellis Son & Vidler, London & Hastings), or a *Vin d'Alsace Kuehn Ammerschwihr Riesling* (Lay & Wheeler Ltd., Colchester) or a *Vin d'Alsace Riesling* (Laytons of Midland Road). *Beaujolais – Burgundy*: Burgundy has become very expensive and it is now fashionable to list it with Beaujolais, even though the two differ widely in character. Burgundies are bigger than their southern cousins and should be kept longer before drinking. Good examples of basic *Mâcon Rouge* are offered by Ellis Son & Vidler, Trevina Meredith Wines Ltd., and Saccone & Speed. *Couronne de Bourgogne N.V.* is a Trevina Meredith wines choice. Both Marks and Spencer and British Home Stores offer a reasonable *Beaujolais*. Peter Dominic has *Le Piat de Beaujolais de Primeur*, an undoubted qualifier for garlic-laden dishes and Trevina Meredith list a lovely big-flavoured *Brouilly*. There are two *Santenays* we recommend: the first is *Domaine de l'Abbaye P. Dumontet* and the second, *Groffier-Leger* – both are fine examples of this lushly beautiful wine (Corney & Barrow, and Hatch Mansfield).

For some suitable white wines, try *Mâcon Blanc Villages, Cuvée Pierre Santé Sommère* and *Sauvignon de St. Bris*, both good value from Ellis Son & Vidler. *Meursault* is a powerhouse wine, as big as its neighbour, *Volnay* (John Harvey & Sons).

Among the red Bordeaux wines (always referred to as claret in England) try *Maitre d'Estournel*, exclusive to Laytons. In *La Capelle*, you have a strong contender in a difficult sector, the generic clarets (Saccone & Speed, Arthur Cooper). *Belair Claret* is another sound choice (H. Sichel & Sons). *Clos du Moulin Haut Medoc* is chateau-bottled (Ellis Son & Vidler) and *Harvey's No. 1 Claret*, an excellent newcomer, is available from John Harvey & Son.

Monopole Dry Blanc de Blanc Bordeaux Blanc Edouard Kressman is a good white Bordeaux (Saccone & Speed).

And what about *Champagne?* Does it make sense to drink this elixir with garlic-dominated dishes? Why not? Many recipes contain champagne *and* garlic! No need to commit yourself to a particular style. This is the view both of a well-known *sommelier* and of the experts in Epernay.

From the Loire region, try *Muscadet*, good for fish and garlicky dishes. A good one is *Muscadet Les Grands Vignobles* (J. & B.), or for a particularly rich example of Vouvray, try John Harvey's one. The sauvignon grape flourishes in this region, so try *Savignon de Touraine*, a particularly beautiful wine obtainable from J. B. Reynier.

The bountiful Mediterranean sun makes the wines of the appellation Côtes de Provence both warm and generous, perfect with Provençal and other cuisines, and good with all garlic feasts. Here is a cross-section of reds: *Chateau de Calavon, Coteaux d'Aix en Provence* (Ellis Son & Vidler); *Chateau Garamache* (Sainsbury's); *Chateau Montaud* (Christopher) and *Chateau la Gardonne* (Woolworth). As for white and rose wines: there is a delicious (and expensive) *Blanc de Blanc clos Mireille* (Domaine Bottled, OTT) produced in a vineyard by the sea; these vineyards have something special about them and their wines go excellently with gourmet-garlic dishes. A new Blanc de Blanc is *Pradel Prestige*, a partner for the already popular rosé, *Pradel Rosé Dry A.C.* The first is made entirely from white grapes and is marginally more expensive than the rosé, but it is also the fairer of the pair, a well-made and balanced wine that is a credit to its region of origin (Peter Dominic).

Rhône wines are perfect for garlic dishes. The vines flourish in the soil of the Rhône, a baked pebbly paradise that produces sunshiny wines gutsy enough to satisfy all garlicky dishes. There are many delicious red wines from this area: *Côtes du Ventoux*, a fruity and easy-to-drink wine (J. B. Reynier); *Côtes du Rhone* (House of Hallgarten); *Tambour Côtes du Rhone* and *Chateau de la Ramiere Côtes du Rhone*, David and Foillard (Saccone & Speed); *Chateauneuf du Pape*, a velvety and powerful wine (Victoria Wine Co.); *St. Joseph* (John Harvey); *Crozes Hermitage* (Trevena Meredith); *Crozes Hermitage* (Hedges & Butler); *Crozes Hermitage Rouge* Estate Bottled (Hallgarten); *Coteaux du Triscastin* (Travena Meredith).

Among the rosés, *Tavel* is the best and most popular. Try *Tavel Rosé, La Fourcadière* (Malmaison Wine Club); *Tavel Rosé* (Hedges and Butler); *Tavel Rosé 'Rhonegarden'* (Hallgarten); *Lirac Rosé* – from an area near Tavel – (Hedges & Butler).

Other French wines are well worth experimenting with: *Menotte Rouge* (Ellis Son & Vidler); *Domaine de Launac* and *Domaine de Truilhas* (the same outlets); *Carcassonne l'Aude Lebeque* and *Fitou A.C. Chantovent* from Languedoc and Roussillon, excellent and modestly priced (Tanners).

Cahors is the famous 'black' wine – not so black as it once was, but still bursting with character (Malmaison Wine Club). *Bandol* produces a wine similar to *Chateauneuf du Pape*, made largely from Mourvedre grapes (same source).

The Dordogne, already well known for its cuisine, is gradually achieving a reputation for its wines. This is an area near Bordeaux, but its wines are much cheaper than most clarets. Tanners stock a good *Bergerac Rouge*, and *Grand Chevalier Rouge* is a red table wine of outstanding quality obtainable from J. B. Reynier.

Among the white wines from this area, and Languedoc and Rousillon try *Hérault Lebeque*, a dry white (Tanners) and *Corfières Blanc* (Stowells, Threshers). Finally consider two authentic litre 'vins ordinaire' produced by the Societé Vinicole G. Doré in Rouen exclusively for Peter Dominic, one white and the other red.

GERMANY   There are a handful of dry German wines which can mix with garlic. Two excellent ones are *Rhine Riesling Dry* and *Franconia Frankenwein Silvaner Dry* – in 'boxbeutal' flagons – both obtainable from Deinhard in London.

GREECE   The wines of modern Greece do not enjoy the prestige of the wines of the ancients; a pity because so many of them are well matched to garlic-scented dishes. *Corinth Red* is a dry wine of ruby colour made from two grapes: the Agios Georgios of Nemea, and the Mavroudi of Kounina. *Corinth White*, from the Peleponnese, is a crisp, dry and delicate wine. *Roditis Rosé* is a dry wine from Patros. *Corinth Retsina* is a white resin wine produced in the same way as any dry white table wine, with the important difference that a few pieces of pine resin are added to the 'must' during fermentation. They are subsequently removed, but the flavour they impart is unmistakable; a highly specialised taste, perfectly suited to garlic dishes and once loved never rejected. All these Greek wines are obtainable from Tzilalis & Co., London.

HUNGARY   The most popular Hungarian wine is *Bull's Blood of Eger* – *Egri Bikavér*. It is a clear, rich, deeply purple wine with a robust and full-bodied character – a successful partner for all spicy dishes (R. & C. Vintners of Norwich and other outlets).

ISRAEL   Israeli wines may not rank among the world's finest; nevertheless the Carmel Wine Co. of London list some creditable wines, among them the *Cabernet Sauvignon* and the *Carmel Avdat Red* – both good red wines for garlic dishes, Israeli or otherwise.

ITALY   Apulia is now making a strong effort to improve the quality of its table wines – formerly Apulian wines were merely constituents of vermouth-type drinks. Look out for *Castel del Monte Rosso D.O.C.*, a deep, spectacular ruby red wine, and *Brindisi Rosso*, as big and bold as you might expect from a wine from this area. *Rosato del Salento* is a very heavy rosé. These three wines were shown at the Italian Trade Centre, Savile Row, London, as were two particularly suitable Lombardy wines:

Barbera Oltrepò Pavese D.O.C. and *Rosso Oltrepò Pavese*. Both are intensely ruby-coloured and full-bodied.

Piedmont has a typically Italian cuisine and generous wines. Try *Barbera delle Langhe*, a dark red wine with plenty of body, or *Barolo Scanavino* and *Barolo Kiolo*, a full-bodied, velvety wine made from the famous Nebbiolo grape (all from Hedges & Butler). Findlaters offer a *Barolo Riserva – Vignaioli*. Another favourite is *Barbares O Vignoto* (Dolamore).

The Roman hills produce *Frascati di Sanctis Amabile*, a strong, medium-sweet wine which works surprisingly well with garlic (Tanners) and *Frascati Secco*, a blend of two grapes, Trebbiano and Malvasia, grown on the hills around Frascati – a crisp, dry wine (Stowells, Threshers).

Roughly speaking, the chianti area of Tuscany is egg-shaped, and at its centre lies a smaller egg shape, from whence comes the superlative wines of Chianti Classico. You can identify these wines by the label showing a black rooster on a gold background with a red border. Among the Chianti Classicos, *Castello Vicchiomaggio* is a fine example (Hunt & Braithwaite). Another is *Classico di Gabbiano* (Ellis Son & Vidler) and *Chianti Classico Montepaldi* (Peter Dominic). For garlic-eating students and others with an eye for a bargain, try *Chianti Barnetti*, a reasonably priced wine supplied in magnums by Augustus Barnett. A delicious Etruscan wine is *La Parrina*, a good, rugged wine produced at Ortobolo near the Tuscan coast. Another is *Fattoria dei Barbi e del Casato*, made from Brunello grapes. The first is from Hunt & Braithwaite and the second is shown at the Italian Trade Centre.

MOROCCO   Tanners of Shrewsbury market an excellent *Moroccan Red* in bottles and litres. Moroccan wines show their French influence; this one is rich but also light.

PORTUGAL   From Dao, *Ribalonga* is a full-bodied and smooth 'winter' red wine, well-suited to garlic dishes (Laytons).

SPAIN   The northwestern vineyards of Spain are called *Rioja*. Here the climate is temperate, the land green, the rain plentiful and the wines of superb quality. All Riojas wines spend a minimum of two years in oak casks – the fine Reservas, ten years. Try any of the following with your choicest garlic recipes: *Red Vina Albina* (Les Amis du Vin); *Marques de Morrieta* (same merchant); *Ederra Rioja* (Saccone & Speed; Arthur Cooper); *Vina Canda, Rioja Tinto* (Dolamore). For a medium dry rosé, try *Lagunilla*, slightly chilled (Peter Dominic) and for an unusual white wine, *Medieval*, with a hint of *Meursault* (Les Amis du Vin). Other Spanish wines, well worth trying: *Castillo de Mudela Red Valdepenas* (Ellis Son & Vidler); *Penedes, Torres Coronas Miguel Torres* and *Vina Sol Miguel Torres* (Malmaison Wine Club).

SOUTH AFRICA Two fine full-bodied dry red wines are *K.W.V. Roodeburg* and *Bertrams* (both from Cape Wine Centre, Great Marlborough Street, London). These are made from the Pinotage grape, a Cape cross between Pinot Noir and Hermitage.

USA From a selection available in Great Britain, try the *Red Pinot Noir*, a medium-bodied wine marketed by Christian Brothers (Harrods; Peter Dominic) and *Beaumont Pinot Noir* from the Beaulieu Vineyard, Napa Valley, California (Avery's of Bristol). Also suitable are *Grignolino*, Heitz Wine Cellars, St. Helena, California (Avery's) and *Petite Sirah Almaden*, imported only by Harvey Prince (Ellis Son & Vidler). *Zinfandel* is a Paul Masson wine imported by Seagram UK. *Cabernet Sauvignon* is obtainable from Peter Dominic and *Cabernet Sauvignon* Martha's Vineyard, a really outstanding, but very expensive wine, and a match for any amount of garlic, from Avery's of Bristol.

Among suitable white wines, there is *Pinot Chardonnay Almaden* (Harvey Prince) and *Pinot Chardonnay* Christian Brothers (Peter Dominic).

YUGOSLAVIA Two fine red wines are *Milion Cabernet Sauvignon* (Les Amis du Vin) – or, without the 'Milion' brand name, obtainable from both Victoria Wine and Sainsbury's – and *Vranac*, a special Yugoslav-bottled red (Widcombe Wine Co., Bath and Les Amis du Vin). There is also a *Milion Riesling* – again, without the brand name, this wine is available from Victoria Wine and Sainsbury's as well as Waitrose and Hall & Woodhouse.

Note on Wines in USA

America imports wine from France, Spain and Italy as well as from many other countries. Not only that: some 30 states produce wines of their own, notable ones coming from New York, Oregon, Maryland and of course, California.

Seven out of every ten bottles of wine Americans drink come from California, a happy state of affairs because Californian wines are superb. Just as Americans' nodding acquaintance with garlic has turned into a robust friendship, so have they forged ahead in their knowledge and appreciation of wine in the last two decades.

87

To help you find wines in the United States comparable to those we have listed here, try the advice of a good wine merchant. There are no nationwide chains such as there are in Great Britain, but we have collected the names of recommended wine shops where you are sure to find assistance in your search for wines to serve with garlic dishes:

New York City
Acker, Merrall & Condit, 2372 Broadway
Astor Wines & Spirits, 12 Astor Place
Cork & Bottle, 1158 First Avenue
Morrell's, 307 East 53rd Street
Quality House, 2 Park Avenue
Sherry-Lehman, 679 Madison Avenue
67 Wine & Spirits, 179 Columbus Avenue
Surrey Liquor, 829 Madison Avenue

Greater New York
Zachy's, 20 Eastern Parkway, Scarsdale
Post's, 536 Jericho Turnpike, Syosset, Long Island
Goldstar, 103 Queens Boulevard, Forest Hills, Long Island
Forest Hills Liquor, 108–110 Queens Boulevard, Forest Hills, Long Island

Arizona
Arcadia Wines, 4513 North Scottsdale Road, Scottsdale

Colorado
Johnnie's Liquors, 1725 South Nevada Street, Colorado Springs
Argonaut Wine & Liquors, 700 East Colfax, Denver

Connecticut
Horsemere Liquor, 25 East Putnam, Greenwich
Town & Country Package, 785 Silver Lane, East Hartford

California
Wine & Cheese Counter, 205 Jackson Street, San Francisco
Beetram's, 1540 El Camino Road, Menlo Park
Corti Brothers, 5760 Freeport Boulevard, Sacramento
Jay-Vee Wines & Liquors, 1316 University Avenue, Berkeley
Pearson's, 2530 San Vincente Boulevard, Santa Monica
The Wine Merchant, 9701 Santa Monica Boulevard, Beverly Hills

Florida
Causeway Liquors, 5479 North Federal Highway, Fort Lauderdale
Foremost Alton Road Liquors, 1683 Alton Road, Miami Beach
Lile's Foremost Liquors, 3162 Commodore Plaza, Coconut Grove

Georgia
McCall's Wine and Cheese Cellars, 3500 Peachtree Plaza, Atlanta
Skinflints, 1260 Winchester Parkway, Smyrna

Hawaii
The Village Market, 1249 Wilden Avenue, Honolulu

Illinois
Poragno's World Wines, 40 East Walton Street, Chicago
Gendler's Wine Cellars, 2518 Fifth Avenue, Rock Island
Malloy's Sarway Stores, Glen Ellyn
Schaefer's Liquors, 9965 Grosse Point Road, Skokie

Louisiana
Martin's Wine Cellars, 3827 Baronne Street, New Orleans

Maryland
Hany's Wine Shop, 3113 Greenmount Avenue, Baltimore

Massachusetts
Harvard Wine and Liquor, 288 Harvard Street, Brookline

Michigan
Village Corner, 601 South Forest, Ann Arbor

Minnesota
Harkell's Liquors, 23 South Seventh Street, Minneapolis
Surdykes, 201 East Hennepin Avenue, Minneapolis

Missouri
905 Liquor Stores, St. Louis

New Jersey
Fine's Spirits, 14 Riveredge Road, Tenafly
Ho-ho-kus Wines & Spirits, 622 Maple Avenue, Ho-ho-kus

North Dakota
Polar Package Place, University Center, 19th Avenue and University Drive, Fargo

Texas
Richards Liquors and Fine Wines, 2124 South Shepher, Houston
Specks, 2410 Smith Street, Houston

Washington, D.C.
Harry's Liquor, Wine and Cheese Shop, 401 M Street SW
Maurice Miller's, 7804 Alaska Avenue, NW
Woodley Liquor, 3423 Connecticut Avenue, NW
Bassins McArthur Liquor, 4877 McArthur Boulevard

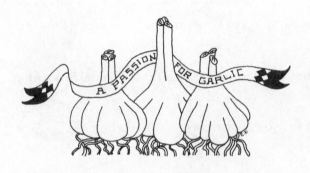

Garlic Miscellany

Victorian Devils

Death-and-damnation devils are not the only ones which flourished in Victorian times – a more palatable devil was the splendidly hot and highly spiced sauce which converted many foods into delectable devilled dishes. Game, turkey, fish, fowl, liver, etc., were marinated in a devilishly hot mixture before cooking. These dishes found favour at breakfast time or as a savoury to climax a dinner.

To make your own devilment:

Ingredients

1 small onion, grated	¼ cup wine vinegar
1 clove garlic, crushed	cayenne pepper, paprika,
1 cup red wine	mustard, chili powder, salt

Method

Marinate the meat in these ingredients for several hours before cooking; turn from time to time so that all surfaces are exposed to the devil. When grilling meat, baste with the mixture.

For a lighter, drier devil, dust meat or fish (sardines are good cooked this way) with garlic powder, dry mustard and pepper and grill for a few minutes before serving.

Devilled Garlic Croutons

To serve with soup, or for compulsive nibbling with sherry or pre-dinner wine: cut up one or two garlic cloves and fry gently in butter.

Sprinkle with paprika and cayenne pepper and then add small squares of white bread and fry them until golden brown. Remove the croutons and drain excess butter on kitchen paper.

Devilled Mushrooms

Peel and trim fresh mushrooms and remove their stalks. Brush the mushrooms outside and inside with melted garlic butter, and then season strongly with salt, cayenne pepper and freshly ground black pepper. Broil for 15 minutes and serve piping hot.

Devilled Tomatoes

Peel firm tomatoes and slice them quite thickly. (The best way to peel a tomato is to pierce it with a fork and hold over a naked gas flame until the skin wrinkles. Plunging them into boiling water, even briefly, makes them too soggy.) Now coat the slices in melted garlic butter and roll them lightly in flour to which you have added a sprinkle of dry mustard. Dust well with black and red pepper. Bake or broil at a brisk heat for about 7 minutes.

(To make a simple garlic butter: in a bowl, press 2–3 garlic cloves and with a fork mix in sufficient butter, up to 4 oz for this amount. The flavour improves if you pack the butter into a small pot, cover closely and store in the fridge.)

Devils on Horseback

You can use fresh or tinned oysters as the Victorians did or as a modern alternative use anchovy fillets as follows: open the tin and remove excess oil by draining and letting tepid water run over the fish. Season each fillet with cayenne and black pepper and dip into melted garlic butter. Wrap each in a very thinly cut slice of fat bacon and skewer with a wooden pick. Lay each fillet on a white-bread crouton which you have fried in garlic butter. Dust with more black pepper and sprinkle with finely chopped chives. Bake in a hot over for 8 minutes until the bacon is cooked. Remove the picks and serve piping hot. These can be served with drinks before dinner, or, as the Victorians did, as an after-dinner savoury.

Devilled Eggs

First prepare this sauce: fry two peeled and thinly sliced garlic cloves in oil until light brown but not burned. Season with a little cayenne pepper and curry powder and continue to stir and cook for a few minutes. Now add ¼ pt basic white sauce seasoned with a few drops of Worcestershire sauce. Stir the mixture thoroughly and pour off any excess fat.

Now fry lightly some thinly sliced ham and dust with red pepper. Cut the slices into strips and line oiled cocottes or small baking cups. Poach one egg for each cocotte, put into the cup and fill to the brim with the devil sauce. Top with a fine layer of grated Parmesan cheese and heat for a few minutes in a hot oven.

Devilled Kidneys

Trim the kidneys (a sharp pair of scissors works best) and slice in two. Dip them in hot melted garlic butter and season with black pepper, cayenne and salt. Broil for about 8 minutes, turning frequently, and serve with a small pat of devil butter on each one. To make devil butter: wash 4 oz butter (squeeze it by hand under cold running water) and work into it with a fork a teaspoon of curry paste, a clove of pressed garlic and a drop of Tabasco sauce.

Devilled Shrimp Canapés

Melt 1 oz garlic butter, add half a pound of cleaned shrimps and dust with a devil seasoning composed of red pepper, black pepper and salt, mixed thoroughly together. Stir the shrimps over a low heat until they have absorbed all the butter. Fry rounds of white bread, about 2½ inches in diameter and ¼ inch thick, in garlic butter. Top with the devilled shrimp sprinkled with finely chopped parsley.

Devilled Biscuits with Cod's Roe

Melt 2 oz of garlic butter in a large frying pan. Arrange 8 water biscuits (or for a luxury touch, 8 Bath Olivers) in the butter so that they do not overlap. Cook on a moderate heat and turn frequently so that they absorb all the butter – but be careful they don't burn. Allow 1 teaspoon

93

of cod's roe for each biscuit. Cook the roe in an ounce of melted garlic butter and then thicken with the beaten yolks of 2 eggs. Spread this mixture over the biscuits, dust with paprika, heat them in the oven for three minutes, and serve super-hot.

Charcuterie

Prepared meats, particularly pork and its conversion into pâtés, hams, salamis and *saucisson*, form the basis of charcuterie. The French do this, as they do other things, superlatively well, but other countries (Italy, Poland, Germany and Spain) also contribute excellent versions. Charcuterie is a clever standby for snacks, starters, school lunches, picnics and parties – or serve it in various forms with salad as a bona-fide meal.

Garlic is an important flavour in charcuterie – the French, Germans and Italians all make garlic sausage and garlic salami. Matteson and Bloom market several varieties in England, and some of the more exotic ones are imported (Fumeé d'Auvergne, Saucisses de Toulouse, Brittany garlic sausage – with and without green peppercorns – and Salami Ardechois).

You can make a simple chicken liver and garlic pâté with half a pound of chicken livers, two or three cloves of garlic, half an onion and two tablespoons of butter, salt and pepper. Cook the chopped garlic and minced onion very slowly in the butter. Do not allow them to brown. Meanwhile clean the livers, removing all the tough skin or tendon – generally not much in chicken livers. Cut the livers into small pieces with a pair of scissors and add the meat to the softened garlic and onion. Cook very slowly until the liver loses its colour, but do not brown. Mash with a fork in the cooking pan to make sure it is thoroughly cooked. Season with salt and pepper. Grind or blend and pack the pâté into a small pot. Chill before serving, and garnish with finely chopped parsley.

Garlic and Cheese

The best garlic cheese is Gaperon, according to Philip Rippon, manager of Paxton and Whitfield, the Jermyn Street cheese specialists. Gaperon was originally a goat's milk cheese from Corsica; now it is made from cow's milk and comes from the Auvergne. It is dome-shaped, garlic-flavoured and superlatively good.

Among the garlicky cream cheeses, Boursin is the best known. Also French, and cheaper, is Margotin. From Ilchester in England comes beer and garlic cheese, a winner on any cheese board. There is also a rennet-curd cheese flavoured with garlic and herbs. Kraft and Marks & Spencer both make a creditable garlic and herb cheese.

You can make your own garlic cheeses by adding minced garlic to plain cream cheese or curd cheese. Begin by mixing the cheese with a little top of the milk until it is smooth. Add the pressed garlic and finely minced parsley and thyme. Beat well. Season with freshly ground black pepper; commercial cream cheeses are usually salty enough, so taste before adding more. Pot and chill.

Add chopped or pressed garlic to grated cheddar cheese, mix well and store in a jar in the refrigerator. Very good on slices of bread for grilling, or as a sandwich filling. Also, coarsely chopped fetta cheese, mixed with garlic and olive oil, is delicious with black olives and fresh sesame seed bread.

A Provençal rarebit: Cover a slice of wholemeal toast with a layer of cheese – Lancashire if you are in England – and lay on top, close together, at least 12 slices of fresh garlic. Toast until the garlic is light brown and the cheese is bubbling hot.

Celery stuffed with a garlic cream cheese and pepper mix makes a refreshing change from roquefort. Wrap the sticks in foil or plastic wrapping and store in the refrigerator for several hours before serving. Dust with paprika.

Garlic and cheese combine well in most cooked cheese dishes: try garlic in leek and cheese pie, savoury cheese soufflé and savoury macaroni cheese. For a supper dish try this:

Mix about a cup of mashed potatoes with grated cheese, hot milk and a crushed clove of garlic. Season with salt and pepper. Now beat in the yolks of two eggs. The mixture should not be too runny – if it is, add a little more mashed potato. Beat the egg whites with a little salt until they are stiff, and fold them into the first mixture. Butter a souffle dish (about $1\frac{1}{2}$ pt size) and gently pour in the potatoes and cheese. Top with a little parmesan cheese and bake in a medium hot oven until the soufflé has risen and is brown on top, about half an hour. Don't forget the garlic.

Garlic with everything

Garlic salt, garlic pepper, garlic granules, garlic powder and minced garlic. You can buy garlic powder in a garlic-shaped container called 'Lazy Garlic', and F. Rochias et Cie produce ground garlic and a garlic-and-parsley mix – useful for vegetables, salads, mussels, etc.

Culpeper produce spice and herb blends – for hamburgers, roast lamb, ham and veal dishes, for kebabs and pilafs, sweet and sour dishes – and there is garlic in every one.

Other firms producing minced, powdered and salted garlic are McCormicks and Schwartz, and an Egyptian firm, Mizan.

Now for the commercial salad dressings: Josephine Terry of London do a gourmet garlic blend, and Kraft make an Italian Garlic Dressing. Good Seasons (USA) produce a salad dressing mix. So do Lawry's (also American); they market at least 6 mixes for seasoning home-made salad dressings and cooked dishes, and a green onion dip mix – all with garlic added.

As for the sauces: Holbrook's Worcestershire Sauce is the No. 1 Man's brand, and HP Sauce, HP Fruity Sauce and Daddies Sauce are dads' and kids' favourites; all are made with garlic, and all are very English. Lea and Perrins Worcestershire Sauce includes garlic as one of its many (some secret) ingredients, and Maggi make a chili and garlic sauce.

By all means keep one or two of these products on the pantry shelf for emergencies; but there are literally no occasions when you cannot use fresh garlic to better effect. In fact, you can make many of the products at home with very little difficulty. Garlic and parsley is a classic example – called *persillade*, you make it by combining very finely chopped fresh parsley with chopped garlic. One of those *Mouli* parsley choppers with the long sharp teeth produce the finest chopped parsley, and you can use your garlic press. Blend the two together for a pungent garnish, especially good on broiled mushrooms, or, mixed with browned bread crumbs, a garlicky topping for roast lamb or roast chicken.

But don't try to freeze garlic at home, either peeled or in its papery covering. It will lose its crisp texture and distinctive pungency. Even when it is an ingredient in a pre-cooked dish which you are freezing for later use, better to add garlic when you are reheating the food before serving. Fresh is always best.

Part II

This Herbe Allium is called Garlecke

This herbe Allium is called Garlecke. The vertue of this herbe is thus. It will unbynde all wycked wyndes within a mannes body. Also it helpeth a man to make water. But it noyeth a mannes eyes bycause of ye great byndynge and drynkynge that it hath vertuously, it drynketh and destroyeth the syght. And also it destroyeth and heleth venym within a man. Also it heleth colde soores as it were treacle. Also it heleth scabbes and marfewes or bladders in what maner place they be in a mannes body, so that it be well froted (rubbed) therewith. This herbe is hote and dry.

from Richard Banckes's *Herbal*, 1525

Four Thieves' Vinegar and the Garlic Cure

No one knows if the following tale is true or mythical. In Marseilles in 1722 there was an epidemic of bubonic plague and four thieves were caught robbing the dead bodies of plague victims. Why didn't they die from plague themselves? Because, they said, they used a potion with vinegar and garlic in it – and not for the first time, garlic was said to perform miracles of antisepsis.

'Four Thieves' Vinegar' took its place among the simples, or herb mixtures, made and used for centuries not only in peasant cottages or country houses but in urban households as well. By the eighteenth century there were hundreds of these recipes, some so ancient that no one knew their origin. Others could be found in herbals, great fat tomes illustrated by woodcuts of herbs, many with elaborate and somewhat rambling instructions for their use. Published by such eminent herbal physicians as John Parkinson and Nicholas Culpeper and reprinted many times, these books were the home doctors for much of the population of England for centuries.

Garlic, the herbalist said, was the remedy for dozens of ailments, conditions and catastrophes. It could cure anything from ringworm to leprosy, from indigestion to earache, from 'the bitings of the mouse called the Shrew' to the bites of mad dogs. If you suffered from spots and blemishes, or 'the falling sicknes', from worms or 'corrupt agues', from 'foul ulcers', or had been poisoned by wolf-bane, hen-bane or hemlock – or if you had jaundice, snakebite, convulsions, or were troubled with deafness, or cramps – for these ailments and dozens more, garlic was the cure.

It is against this background of folk medicine and miracle cure that contemporary medical research teams set out to evaluate garlic as a medicine. Today they are at work in hospitals and laboratories all over the world – there is scarcely a major country without at least one project underway. The advantages of finding and developing a 'natural' or plant therapy in countries where chemical medicines are expensive to manufacture and difficult to procure are obvious. But even scientists in the developed countries are intrigued by the qualities of garlic; since 1915 there has been a marked increase in the number of serious research projects concerning its therapeutic value and the results of well over a hundred of them have already been published, many in Great Britain and the United States.

What diseases and conditions are under investigation? Almost every ailment in the herbalists' catalogues – leprosy and skin cancers are two examples – plus a few not identified until fairly recently. Foremost among dozens of projects, however, must be the ones most intriguing to a panacea-seeking public: those concerned with cholesterol in the blood, leading to arteriosclerosis or hardening of the arteries; and hypertension or high blood pressure. Indian and German doctors in particular have been active in their investigations into the effect of garlic oil in experimental cholesterol atherosclerosis, as well as in their research into garlic's antibacterial properties.

Ten years ago experiments in India and Libya established beyond doubt that the essential oil in garlic – a sulphurous, volatile oil – could be isolated and that in addition to 'that smell', it had a measurable and destructive effect upon the fatty particles in the blood. Good news, for as every reader of the small print in margarine advertisements knows, it is the build-up of these particles which leads to coronary heart disease, stroke and hardening of the arteries.

To test the hypothesis, English breakfasts of bacon and eggs, foods rich in cholesterol, were fed to five healthy individuals, followed by doses of garlic juice and the extracted essential oil of garlic. When the subjects' blood was tested, it did not contain the amounts of cholesterol usually present after fatty foods have been eaten.

At about the same time, in 1969, a researcher reported in the *Lancet*, the journal of the British Medical Association, that five consecutive cases of hypertension had had the level of their blood pressure reduced after being given garlic.

Since then tests such as these have been repeated in many different laboratories and hospitals. In Libya, garlic was fed to rabbits and again it was found effective in inhibiting the increase in cholesterol.

We might with reason now ask whether the medical profession, reading about these and other equally surprising results, responded by flinging away all its conventional medicines and techniques for dealing with high blood pressure or suspected coronary heart disease. The answer must be no; but neither would it be fair to say that only scoffing, ridicule and disbelief have been the portion of the medical researcher.

More and more doctors, as they become familiar with the favourable results of current research, are coming to accept the fact that garlic contains constituents of great value in the treatment of some illnesses. For example, it is now recognised as a reasonably effective antibiotic – not as powerful as some, but without uncomfortable or damaging side effects; nor has there been any report of individuals building up an immunity to it.

Garlic is also recognised as a good antiseptic. During the First World War, surgeons who had to perform operations away from supplies of conventional antiseptics used garlic juice and sphagnum moss to cleanse wounds; the results were excellent. Garlic is also called 'Russian penicillin'; Russian doctors use it to treat tubercular infections. It is also acknowledged to be a good expectorant, loosening heavy phlegm in bronchitis and helping victims of asthma and emphysema to breathe more freely, and it has diuretic and diaphoretic qualities – that is, it encourages urination and perspiration.

As for the more complicated conditions, those which involve the composition of the blood, its circulation and consistency, some specialists – haematologists and clinicians interested in the treatment of coronary artery diseases – are increasingly aware that garlic contains constituents which can, once they are made accessible through distillation or synthesis, play an important role in treatment.

The most valuable compounds in garlic, those which act upon the clotting rate of blood, need much more research if their functions are to be properly understood. Garlic contains 0.1 to 0.3 per cent of a volatile (that is, an evaporating) oil containing allyl propyl disulphide and diallyl disulphide. These are the sulphurous compounds, and sulphur is the ingredient in fresh garlic which makes it smell – as someone has said – 'like onion twenty times'. Efforts to isolate odourless therapeutic properties in garlic have recently been made, but so far tests of their effectiveness are inconclusive.

Perhaps the best hope that the healing properties in garlic will be made more widely available lies in the possibility that chemists will develop methods for isolating and preparing the essential oil in an odourless and tasteless form. Garlic is not today's 'miracle cure' – for anything. It would be closer to the truth to say that, when it is fresh, it contains valuable therapeutic qualities which we would be unwise to ignore. We will help ourselves by learning to accept it as an unusually bountiful gift of nature – a plant easy to grow in almost any climate, whose usefulness will be increasingly recognised for a great number of medical purposes.

NOTE

Some of the information in this section comes from an article by H. A. Dewar, MD, FRCP, in the January 1978 issue of the British *Journal of Pharmacotherapy*. Dr Dewar's article, 'Onions, garlic and the circulatory system', will be interesting both to layman and specialist. In it he describes some of the work that has been done by clinical researchers, and adds a thoughtful and sensible account of lessons to be learned from investigating plant materials as medicines for treating conditions of the blood.

We are also indebted to Dr Hans Reuter of the Medizinische Universitatsklinik, Cologne. A victim of the Miracle Cure myth, Dr Reuter received world-wide publicity following a misleading newspaper report about his work with garlic in the autumn of 1978. He patiently replied to requests for information with a carefully written account of his own research into the platelet inhibiting effects of garlic extracts, and included an article he has written in *Der Deutsche Apotheker* (June 1978) on the uses of garlic and garlic extracts as medicaments. He was also good enough to supply a list of 97 research projects into the therapeutic uses of garlic.

Possibly the most unexpected use to which garlic has been put is revealed in a journal not easily obtainable in the West. W. C. Hsu contributed an article to the *Chinese Medical Journal* (May 1977) entitled 'Garlic slice used in repairing eardrum perforation'.

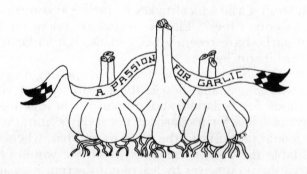

'Take nine cluffa garleaces ...'

Prescriptions for taking garlic as a medicine, when one reads them in herbals ancient or modern, do not always inspire confidence. 'Take nine cluffa garleaces' begins one: rather a large dose even for the desperate maladies prevalent in A.D. 1000, when it was written, and surely excessive today.

Contemporary herbals are not much more helpful – some, though they are less explicit, leave you with the feeling that their belief in the efficacy of garlic is based more upon folklore than fact. One dauntless writer suggests taking one to six cloves of garlic two or three times a day, and swallowing them without chewing.

Raw garlic is not one of those remedies one can take with a light and careless heart – not like, say, aspirin, which we are inclined to take without much thought – not a good idea, but not a difficult thing to do. But the taking of garlic must be done in an entirely different spirit: with conviction, determination and resolve. In short, you have to be sure you really mean it. Nothing tasting like raw garlic can be used in any other way.

Nor can you put cloves of garlic in your pocket and munch on them as you pursue your daily life – not, that is, in most parts of the United States or Britain. It is true that something like a craze for taking garlic 'for your health' has been noted here and there around the world; it has been reported in places as far apart as Bombay and New York. Even so, the practice cannot be said to be so popular or widespread that your entrance into a gathering bearing about you fumy clouds of garlic will go unnoted and uncriticised. No, if the dose you select requires you to take your garlic at times when you are away from home, you will have to use foresight. Provide yourself with a toothbrush, or cumin seeds to chew, or a sprig of fresh parsley, the oldest antidote of them all. The early herbalists thought that chewing a fresh green bean was the most effective means of reducing the smell of garlic, but any fresh herb – thyme or mint are both good – will mask the odour.

Although it is odourless when left undisturbed in its papery covering, garlic releases its characteristic pungency as soon as you cut into the flesh of the clove. Naturally, the idea of an odourless but potent garlic, converted into more conventional forms of medicines, is an appealing one, but at present there are no reliable synthesised forms of garlic available to the public which duplicate the active constituents of fresh garlic, nor is the encapsulated garlic oil, now widely available in health food shops, the same as the active, volatile material you press from the garlic clove.

Höfels, one of the largest suppliers of garlic oil in Britain – everything 'from Pearles for humans to liquid for race-horses' – have been producing an especially potent cold-press garlic oil for a Medical Research Council grant-aided project into cholesterol in the blood being conducted by researchers in a north London Hospital. It will be a happy day for us all if the research is successful in showing that this oil can lower blood cholesterol safely, and that it can be made available to the public without risk. Until we know, it is better to use freshly pressed garlic for medicinal purposes than any garlic tablet, powder or capsule. These last are called, quite accurately, dietary supplements.

There are good reasons for you to investigate the possibility of taking garlic for your health, and for discovering how much to take, how often to take it, and in what form. If you suffer from high blood pressure, the prospect of being able to lower the pressure to a reasonable level by taking a vegetable as medicine must be pleasing, especially if it means that you can abandon chemical medicines, some of which can produce distressing side-effects. But you must engage the cooperation of your doctor once you have decided to try garlic for this purpose; it would be extremely foolhardy to abandon the conventional medication you have been prescribed for a serious chronic condition, without your doctor's knowledge and help.

The best and easiest way to take fresh garlic is to use a press. You don't need to peel the clove. Simply express the material into a small cup, add a few tablespoons of milk – not icy cold but at room temperature – mix garlic and milk together, and drink it all down. If you prefer a savoury dose, decant a tin of jellied consommé into a clean screw-top jar and use one or two tablespoonsful, keeping the rest in the refrigerator for future use. The first few times you may find the potion difficult to take; it is delicious only to the initiate. Best to take a deep breath and down it in one go. (And use a metal press – plastic ones are useless.)

You can also spread the freshly pressed garlic on a slice of bread and butter and eat it – not as efficient and definitely more fattening (although garlic itself has only 5 calories per clove). If obesity is not your problem, you can add various flavourings: try honey and garlic, or garlic with cream cheese, cottage cheese or plain yoghurt.

A particularly delicious way to take your garlic is to sprinkle a piece of bread liberally with olive oil and slice or press the garlic on top. Olive oil isn't as fattening as other oils and butters; it seems to assist the metabolism. With a glass of wine, this must be the least painful way to take 'medicine' ever devised. It is also known as 'the Greek shepherd's breakfast'.

Whatever vehicle you choose, don't take too long to prepare your dose; the freshness dissipates very quickly, and with it, the benefit.

How often should one take this dose? To begin with, once a day, preferably in the morning. The beginner may prefer taking it in the evening, with a night's lapse to make sure there are no fumes for the next day. After a few days, increase your intake to twice daily. W. A. R. Thomson, editor of *Healing Plants, a Modern Herbal*, (London 1978), recommends the sensible dose of one clove 'several times a day' for several weeks for arteriosclerosis; but it seems reasonable also to assume that you will need to take it even longer. He suggests the same dose – that is, one clove taken two to three times a day for several months – to combat high blood pressure. The duration of the treatment must depend upon the results; your doctor will be able to tell you whether your blood pressure has responded satisfactorily, but even if you should be disappointed in this, you will be assisting your general health – digestion, for example, is usually much improved.

Some time ago, doctors in India noted that toxemia in pregnant women could be treated successfully with garlic. If you are pregnant you may like to try taking one or two cloves of garlic each day; garlic is a well-known diuretic, and the swellings in knees and ankles which can cause discomfort in pregnancy may well be lessened by this treatment. Again, it would be unwise to substitute garlic for medicines given you by your doctor without consultation with him.

French race-horses are fed garlic and onions if they suffer from swollen joints or blood clots. It might be worth a try if you yourself suffer from rheumatism or arthritis. Garlic will very likely help you, and certainly won't harm you.

If you are treating adolescent outbreaks of pimples or boils, you will have the greatest chance of success with those on the back. For this treatment, mix crushed garlic with a bland vehicle such as lard, or add it to a paste of cornflour and water, and apply directly to the affected areas. Don't put raw garlic mixtures near the eyes; it can sting and burn. To treat pimples on the face, take fresh garlic by mouth. It is a good "blood purifier' – that is, it contains antibiotic material – so a regimen of two to three cloves by mouth every day for at least two weeks should yield gratifying results.

Garlic also makes a useful poultice, to bring down localised swellings, or to draw out infection. Crush a clove of garlic on to a clean piece of muslin and cover with another piece. Grease the affected area lightly and lay the poultice on top.

You can make an effective linctus or cough mixture for adults who suffer from asthma, bronchitis or emphysema. Mix one crushed clove of garlic with honey, syrup or fruit jelly. This was one of the doses our Victorian grandparents gave to children suffering from whooping cough, but modern research has shown that it is dangerous to give raw garlic or raw garlic preparations to very young children. Instead, try one of the old remedies: put a clove of garlic, peeled, into each of the child's shoes; or mix crushed garlic with lard and spread the mixture on the soles of the feet at night, covering with a pair of cotton socks.

Not surprisingly, therapeutic garlic has thrown up a few eccentrics and enthusiasts in its long history. Garlic seems to encourage hyperbole. Most garlic devotees lead quiet lives writing about their panacea in pamphlets and obscure journals. For instance, there is a paper called 'The Garlic Times' now published in California, devoted entirely to garlic news.

One effective contemporary advocate of garlic is Juliette de Bairacli-Levy who has written a number of books in which she tells how to use herbs to treat ailments in animals. In her books she gives many garlic recipes for treating diseases of the nose, throat and intestines of dogs, horses and various farm animals, recommending concoctions and infusions which lower fevers, act as vermifuges and heal wounds and sores.

Perhaps the most arresting bit of information occurs in her handbook for farm and stable. Here she reports confidently that 'gorillas frequently plant areas of garlic where they have their colonies'. Gorillas frequently planting garlic! We live in a better world than we knew.

Another endearing garlic enthusiast is a Japanese named Yoshio Kato, author of a little book called *Garlic: The Unknown Miracle Worker*. Not if Mr. Kato can help it. His company, the Oyama Garlic Laboratory in Amagasakici, has developed an odourless garlic medicine and a method for using it that borders on the bizarre. The patient first takes a dry thermal bath, a sort of Japanese sauna, to open the pores for what comes next. Then he is enclosed (except for the head) in a special chamber and sprayed all over from a multitude of showers with the garlic medicine solution. The rest of the treatment consists of more showers and applications of the medicine to specific parts of the body, to cure a variety of ailments – athlete's foot, and neuralgia, and ringworm, and frostbite.

There are pictures of the garlic shower cabinet in Mr. Kato's pamphlet, and one of Mr. Kato himself looking very healthy indeed and extremely serious.

Practitioners of homoeopathic medicine believe that every individual has a total mental and physical constitution which, when an illness strikes, must be the object of the doctor's careful study. When he feels he understands the patient's character, and why he has been afflicted with a particular ailment, the doctor is ready to prescribe the remedy that he feels best suits the patient.

To the homoeopathic physician, garlic is a remedy suitable only for certain sorts of people. The fleshy (fat?) individual with a tendency to dyspepsia and catarrhal ailments will benefit from the minute amounts of infused garlic which are typical of the homoeopathic prescription. It is not a remedy recommended for vegetarians.

The *Herbal Pharmacopoeia*, for the use of herbal physicians and chemists, describes and analyses garlic in terms comparable with the definition and description in the pharmocopoeias of conventional medicine, and explores thoroughly the uses to which dried, tinctured and syrup garlic may be put. It has a wide spectrum of uses, from chronic bronchitis to respiratory catarrh, recurrent colds, whooping cough, bronchitic asthma and influenza – and is a valued adjunct to the herbal doctor's medicine chest.

Not so very long ago, the western world was told that yoghurt was the secret behind those incredibly long-lived people from obscure Russian and Balkan villages. (It is so quiet in some of those villages, with only the rare photographer and journalist to raise the blood pressure, that even yoghurt must seem a gustatory delight.) Can it be that longevity in the Balkan countries is due, instead, to garlic? For their ingestion of this healthy plant is higher than almost anywhere in the world. It would be fascinating to know if the rate of arteriosclerosis and cardiac infarction is lower in the Balkans, or in Italy – where they eat great quantities of garlic and have never, at least by one observer, been seen to drink yoghurt at all.

How to Know and Grow Garlic

Garlic is easy to grow – in your garden, in window boxes or in pots. Experienced gardeners can plant a row of garlic in the spring in the same way that onion sets are planted: in clean, well-drained soil with plenty of humus in a sunny part of the vegetable garden, using stock from a reputable supplier. Plant the cloves or 'garlic seed' (not true seeds but very small bulbs) 1½ inches deep, about 5 inches apart and with 12 to 18 inches between the rows. For every 25 feet you plant, you can expect to harvest about 10 pounds of garlic bulbs.

Lift the bulbs in late summer when the leaves begin to turn yellow and dry them in any airy place, tying the long stalks and leaves together while they are still supple. Don't put off your harvest too long or the stem may rot (especially in a wet summer) or it may become too brittle to tie attractively. Cut off any seed heads as they appear or the plant will send its growth to them; the stem bearing the seeds will thicken and the underground bulbs remain small and useless.

New gardeners can begin by planting those cloves of garlic which came already sprouting from the greengrocer's, or which softened and began to show green tips when we weren't looking. Experienced gardeners, of course, are not excluded from this method of acquiring planting stock.

If you are going to plant garlic which has already begun to sprout, first divide the bulb into its individual cloves. There can be as many as 20 of these clustered around a central core or stalk. The outside ones, just under the papery covering, are larger than the inner ones and are certain to yield composite bulbs when planted. The smaller, inside cloves sometimes produce single bulbs in maturity rather than the usual cluster, but these will revert to the composite form during the next growing season; so plant and harvest the small cloves at the same time as the large ones, storing both kinds of bulb for the next time of planting.

Garlic is a good subject to include in your window-box herb garden, or to plant in pots, whether indoors or out. Two cloves to a medium-sized pot will do. Be sure to provide good drainage. Use one of the potting mixtures, or even some ordinary garden earth, and plant each clove just below the surface. You can raise garlic plants indoors at any time of the year – a windowsill where there is some sunshine is best. The fresh green top growth is delicious in salads or added to cottage cheese as a change from chives; it is somewhat milder in flavour than the bulb. Cut away only one or two leaves from your plants if you also wish them to develop into bulbs, and don't over-water. Garlic doesn't like wet feet.

If you plant garlic outdoors in March, in most temperate climates you can expect to harvest your crop in the autumn, when the leaves begin to turn yellow. You don't need to 'cure' the bulbs: they can be stored either in wire baskets or in strings. In warmer climates you can make two plantings. There is a bonus when you plant garlic, for the 'flower' of the garlic stalk produces, not seeds, but miniature bulbs, and these, when planted, produce composite bulbs just as the large cloves do. Seedsmen sometimes sell them as garlic 'seed' – but of course they are not. You can use these tiny bulbs in cookery – whole or crushed – and their flavour is as strong as garlic cloves.

Some gardeners, even very experienced ones, believe that cultivated garlic is too delicate to withstand low temperatures in winter. But S. K. Dark, writing about her experiences in Oklahoma tells us, in an article in *Organic Gardening and Farming* for January 1978, that in her opinion garlic must be one of the most over-priced vegetables in the world because it is 'about as difficult to grow as crab grass'. Annoyed to discover that she had paid an exorbitant price for one decayed and one sprouting bulb, Ms Dark determined to try and grow her own. She planted the cloves from the bulb which had sprouted, an inch down in her garden, and forgot all about them from August until the following March. It was time to plant onions when she noted that the neglected cloves were showing new growth. 'In early June, each plant sent up a long, corkscrew shoot. As the days passed, the shoot slowly unwound until a long seed-head (*sic*) of bulblets bobbed chest-high in the breeze' (– but then, the corn in Oklahoma does grow as high as the eye of an elephant).

The first crop was harvested that autumn when the long green leaves had wilted. She saved the bulblets, spreading them on a freshly turned plot of soil and raking some compost over them. By the following midsummer, her 'seedlings' were thick as new grass, so she transplanted them here and there around her garden – some under trees, others in odd corners. That was the beginning. She now uses only bulblets for planting, saving the composite bulbs for her own use, or to give to friends. She harvests 10 pounds of garlic a year. The bulblets are planted in July, and spend the winter in temperatures well below zero.

What kind of plant is it that produces flower-borne bulbs instead of seeds? Botanists say that garlic is a member of the lily family (Liliaceae) – an unstable family, botanically, because it has a great many varying characteristics. Some of its 500 members or varieties are sweet-scented and ornamental garden plants, while others are the onions and shallots, the leeks and chives – and the garlics. There are at least twenty different kinds of garlic, but the best known is *Allium sativum* – cultivated garlic. It grows to a height of from 18 to 20 inches in most climates, sometimes taller. Its leaves have veins running in straight lines from top to bottom; they look much like the leaves of ordinary grass although they are somewhat softer and less rigid.

A. sativum also has a stalk, called a scape, at the top of which a casing or spathe develops which in time opens to reveal the umbel. This is a thick spray of little flowering heads, usually white but sometimes pale green or light purple. The miniature bulbs, called bulblets or bulbils, develop from the umbel and can be planted in the same way that one plants true seeds.

Some of the other Alliums, or garlics, grow in particular parts of the world, or in particular environments; others have an enormous range. There is one called *A. ampeloprasum*, great-headed or Levant garlic, traces of which were found when Jericho was excavated. Another is *A. ursinum*, bear's garlic or ramsons, a broad-leaved variety considered by farmers to be one of a number of 'serious weeds' because dairy cattle eat them when browsing and the milk is tainted; so is the flesh of beef stock. *A. vineale*, crow's garlic, is another variety. Pollinated by insects, it grows 1,500 feet up in the Yorkshire dales, and has spread throughout southern and eastern England. Crow's garlic also appears as far north as Aberdeen in Scotland; it is found in Ireland, Scandinavia, the Channel Islands, in the southwestern parts of the Soviet Union and in the Crimea; and in Sardinia, Sicily, Macedonia and the Lebanon.

A. canadense, Canadian garlic, flourishes in the northeastern parts of North America; the Indians used to boil and eat the bulbs. *A. chinense* is cultivated in China and Japan, where it is made into pickle for export. Travellers in Hongkong and Bangkok have reported that a single-bulb garlic, usually brown or purple in colour, is sold in the street markets.

Rocambole (*A. scorodoprasum*) sometimes called Spanish garlic or sand garlic, doesn't have the strong odour or taste of ordinary garlic. Because its scape turns and twists, it has been called serpent's garlic. It has an undivided bulb with a purple skin; its umbel and bulbils are also purple. Peeled and sliced, the bulb adds a pleasant flavour of garlic to salads without its bite. Planting stock can be bought from specialist seedsmen – they call it either elephant, jumbo or giant garlic, and one catalogue describes a variety which grows to a diameter of six inches.

There are some beautiful garlics, fine enough to include in a wild garden or shrubbery. Golden garlic, *A. moly*, is one. It can grow in almost any environment and in any kind of soil, and provides a welcome glow of colour according to one specialist; but he recommends putting it in a shady nook – not everyone appreciates its scent.

You will have to beware of a few rather sinister-sounding diseases and pests if you grow garlic in your garden. Stem and bulb eelworm are hazards, and white rot and various other virus ailments also sometimes strike. Clean soil and adequate drainage are both essential to healthy growth; garlic doesn't like soil that is heavy and wet.

But garlic is itself a vital ingredient in some home-made remedies for controlling garden pests. Here is a recipe for a kind of soup made from garlic cloves, marigold flowers and chives: In a saucepan put 6 garlic cloves, a dozen marigold flowers and a good handful of chives. Cover the ingredients with water and bring to a boil. Turn off the heat when the mixture is boiling, but let the brew stand for at least an hour. Strain off the liquid and dilute with 4–5 parts of water; stir well, and use as a spray against blight, aphids, sucking bugs and mosquito larvae. You can also pack your blender with the same ingredients, adding enough water to make a good mix. Strain the resulting puree and add 2 or 3 spoonfuls of the liquid to 32 fluid ounces of water; mix well and spray.

Herbal mixtures such as this one have more than tradition to recommend them. The ability of garlic solutions to kill the larvae of the Culex mosquito was reported in 1971 in the journal *Science*, published in Washington, D.C., while the London *New Scientist* in 1977 printed a paper describing how garlic was being used to fight bean disease.

'My late good Father always set a row of onions between every row of carrots,' writes a County Cork contributor to a useful book called *Gardener's Folklore*, written by Margaret Baker (Newton Abbot 1977). Garlic would do just as well; it is an excellent companion plant, not only for carrots but for onions as well. A New Zealand gardener reports that he planted garlic around four rose bushes heavily infested with black spot; as the garlic grew, the black spot vanished. The University of California Entomological Research Station confirms that garlic is also effective against pests which afflict raspberries and grapes. Another experimenter planted alternate rows of garlic and onions and, over a three-year period, 98 per cent of the crop was free of onion fly.

But of course most people do not grow garlic, either for themselves or as companions for their plants. They buy it.

Garlic is a cash crop in many countries. Spain, Egypt, France, Italy, Argentina, Brazil, the United States and Mexico grow most of the world's crop; Japan, China, Greece and India, as well as Rumania, Bulgaria and Poland, also grow substantial quantities. Much of the garlic crop is consumed in the country of origin, particularly in the countries around the Mediterranean.

Great Britain hardly ranks as a world producer of garlic: production in 1979 was not expected to exceed 20 hectares (about 50 acres). The National Specialist in Vegetable Crops for the Ministry of Agriculture, Fisheries and Food, E. C. Herwin, says that the amount of garlic being grown in England is steadily increasing, especially in the southern counties. Quite possibly more is being produced than is reported, perhaps in country gardens where vegetables are grown for sale in local markets.

The British find garlic faintly amusing as a vegetable crop; it never fails to feature in newspaper headlines if there is a strike of lorry drivers and no vegetables are brought to market, or if for any other reason there is a shortage of fresh vegetables. 'A small, French-looking man scurried out of the new Covent Garden market in Nine Elms, London, yesterday, carrying two hundred-weight bags of garlic cloves – enough to keep a bistro in flavouring until next May ...' – this from the *Guardian*, 5 January 1979, when the city was in the grip of freezing snow storms.

There is at present an experimental 12-month scheme to help Ugandan Asians in England to acquire the necessary expertise to enable them to grow their own 'exotic' vegetables, financed by a grant from the Manpower Services Commission. Ten vegetables were proposed for this scheme, including aubergines, sweet and hot peppers, mustard seeds and ginger; but no prizes for guessing which 'exotic' vegetable featured in a headline in the *Daily Telegraph*: '£100,000 for Garlic Growers'.

In France they arrange matters more seriously. There is a *Comptoir de l'Industrie d'Ail* to advise and encourage growers. The French grow garlic in almost every part of the country. Six thousand hectares were devoted to it in 1978 and 40,000 tonnes were produced in that year. They also imported 8,667 tonnes – and exported 3,888. Prices vary with the season but the crop brought in an average of something over 7F per kilo during the year.

The United States produced a crop valued at 16 million dollars in 1977 – half of it was exported (572 hundred-weight) and another 18½ million dollars' worth was imported. So the average American family apparently ate about 40 cents worth of garlic in that year – not, perhaps, an amount signifying passion, but then many American gardeners now grow their own.

112

While passionate garlic lovers may prefer the home-grown bulbs, or the fresh ones bought at the market, consider a few of the garlic products now available – sometimes for specific uses, and sometimes simply better than nothing. There are garlic powders and garlic granules, garlic salts and garlic oils. Turn to p. 96 for a comprehensive and reassuring guide to products containing garlic; you need never be without it again.

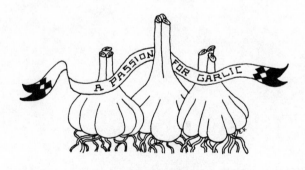

Part III

A Little Garlic Anthology

Devil's posy, poor man's treacle,
heal-all, môly …

A Little Garlic Anthology

Love and Hate

Sith Garlicke then hath powre to save from death
Beare with it though it make unsavoury breath;
And scorne not garlicke like to some that thinke
It only makes men winke, and drinke, and stinke
Hartington, The Englishman's Doctor, 1607

It is reported that in 1368, Alphonse, King of Castile, who had an extreme repugnance to garlic, instituted an order of knighthood; and one of the statutes was, that any knight who had eaten of this plant, could not appear before the sovereign for at least one month.
Alexis Soyer

PARDON ME. Sir – I do not know whether I am getting more sensitive or whether more garlic is being used both here and on the Continent, but could not restaurateurs everywhere be persuaded to provide 'garlic free' rooms like the railways do non-smoking compartments?
G. Izmidlian, letter to the Daily Telegraph, 13 November 1978

He (Günter Grass) is a good cook who prepares at least half the family meals. A necessary part of the education of his children was to teach them to lard a leg of mutton with garlic.
Interview in the Observer, 1 October 1978

Garlic, which is excellent as a flavouring to most sauces, is such a dangerous thing to use in a kitchen that the way I manage it is this: put 5 or 6 cloves of garlic in a wide-necked bottle and cover them with good spirits of wine. When wanted, stick a skewer or fork into the spirit and use a drop or two. The spirit evaporates and the flavour of the garlic

117

remains. But even in this way it must be used carefully for English palates ...

Mrs Earle, *Pot-pourri from a Surrey Garden*, 1899

This olde opinion you may teach your Brother,
How one good Odour is contrary to another;
But it is not soe of stinking smells,
For stinch of Garlick voydeth stinch of Dunghills.

Norton, *Ordinal*, 1472

I had rather live with cheese and garlic in a windmill ...

Shakespeare, *Henry IV*, Part 1

Enlightened young men, who in the thirties published slim leatherbound volumes of verse, now run garlic and fishnet restaurants in SW3.

Clement Freud, *Freud on Food*, 1978

We remember the fish, which we did eat freely; the cucumbers, and the melons, and the leeks, and the onions, and the garlick.

Numbers 11:5

If your mother is an onion, and your father garlic, how could your smell be sweet, poor chap.

A Cairene proverb

Some hours after eating this dish (it contains 20 cloves of garlic) there is a peculiar sensation of liberation in the head, and it is as if one had acquired a completely new sense of smell.

Patience Gray and Primrose Boyd, *Plats du Jour*, 1957

King Baudon: Now say, Huart, as God is your judge, what kind of food do you like the most? I shall know if you are telling me the truth.

Huart: Good rump of pork, heavy in fat, with strong nut and garlic sauce. I ate so much the other day it turned my bowels upside down.

Robin and Marion, by Adam de la Halle, a 13th-century troubadour.

We absolutely forbid it entrance into our Salleting by reason of its intolerable Rankness, and which made it so detested of old that the eating of it was part of the Punishment for such as had committed the horrid'st Crimes.

John Evelyn, 1699

Herodotus says the Scythians eat garlic, and that they are 'a fat and humorous people'.

Anon.

To find a name for me the gods took care
A mystic name that might my worth declare.
They call me Moly: dull Grammarian's sense
Is puzzled with the term,
But Homer held Divine intelligence.
In Greek and Latin both my name is great
The term is just, but Moly sounds more neat
My powers prevented Circe's dire design;
Ulysses but for me had been a swine.
In vain had Mercury inspir'd his brain
With craft, and tipped his wheedling tongue in vain,
Had I not enter'd timely to his aid.

Anon.

Wel loved he garleck, oynons, and eek leekes,
And for to drynken strong wyn, reed as blood.
Chaucer, The Canterbury Tales

If ever any man with impious strangle an aged parent, may he eat of garlic, deadlier than the hemlock! Ah! what tough vitals reapers have! What venom this that rages in my frame? Has vipers' blood without my knowledge been brewed into these herbs? Or has Canidia tampered with the poisonous dish? When Medea was enraptured with the hero Jason, fair beyond all the Argonauts, 'twas with this she anointed him, as he essayed to fasten upon the steers the unfamiliar yoke; 'twas with presents steeped in this, that she took vengeance on her rival and fled on her winged dragon. Never o'er parched Apulia did such heat of dog-star brood, nor did Nessus' gift burn with fiercer flame into the shoulders of Hercules, that wrought mighty deeds. But if ever, my merry Maecenas, you wish to repeat the jest, I pray your sweetheart may put her hands before your kisses, and lie on the farthest edge of the couch.

Horace, Epode 3

119

To ward off ghosts: rub a person all over with garlic which has been crushed to a paste, while you make the sign of the cross. Also, if you suspect a dead person of having been a witch, place a clove of garlic in her mouth.

Romania

In Stoke-on-Trent in 1973, an unfortunate Pole who was in great fear of being attacked by vampires while he slept, died from ingesting a whole garlic clove in his sleep. Garlic was found in the corners of his room.

England

Garlic will destroy monsters.

Hindu saying

Hang garlic near the doorposts of your kitchen where fairies are prone to interfere with the activity of churning butter ... and in the baby's cradle to thwart evil 'fairy' godmothers who might take your child and leave a changeling.

Dictionary of Symbols and Imagery, 1974

The restless souls of heretics, criminals and suicides take the form of bats and leave their burial places at night to drink human blood. They can be identified because they cast not shadow, are not reflected in mirrors and can only rest when they have been staked through the heart or have had their daytime hiding-places destroyed. A necklace of garlic can prevent vampires from doing their foul worst.

Originally a Slavic legend, written as a tale by the
Irish writer Bram Stoker in *Count Dracula*, 1897

To drive out evil spirits when a cow develops black leg: make a small incision, insert a clove of garlic and sew up the wound with one stitch.

Ireland

The bullfighters of the Aymora Indians wear it believing if the bull smells it, he will not charge.

Dictionary of Folklore, 1972

In Bulgaria, envious persons are thwarted in their bad wishes by the hanging of a garlic plant over the door. If this fails, garlic is rubbed on all the pans and kettles in the house; this thoroughly routs any evil thoughts out of the home.

Encyclopedia of Superstitions, 1903

Bizi Ko vistica od bilaga luka ... She runs from it like a witch from white garlic.

Romany Gypsy

Tibetan monks and nuns are forbidden to eat garlic because it is believed to be followed by ill luck.

Anon.

In some villages it is the custom to smear the doors of the stables with garlic and valerian on the night of St George to prevent witches from suckling cows.

Romania

Remedies and Cures

Garlic simmered in hen broth cures constipation.

Medieval prescription

To cure bronchitis in children: chop the leaves and cloves finely, lay between brown paper and use as a poultice on the chest.

Ireland

All the root bulbs have drawing power, and garlic or onion tied to corns can ease the pain. Many ancient herbal books mention roasted clove of garlic used several nights in a row as a cure for corns.

Dian Dincin Buchman, *Feed Your Face*, 1973

Ail ... une proprieté curieuse d'ail, bien connue des soldats et des prisonniers desireaux d'être admis a l'infirmerie, c'est qu'une gousse introduite dans le rectum peut determiner un acces de fièvre passager.

La Grande Encyclopedie, Paris, 1887

Garlicke ... with figge leaves and Cumin it is laid on against the bitings of the Mouse.

Gerard

Garlick makes a man slepe.

Stanbridge, *Vulgaria*, 1509

121

Cocks fed on garlic are most stout to fight, and so are Horses. (If your garden is infested with moles) garlic will make them leap out of the ground presently.

Cole, *Art of Simpling*, 1543

If a goose be eaten above four months old, it is badly digested without garlic sauce, exercise and strong drink.

Thomas Monfet, 1542

To worm a dog: put an unpeeled garlic clove in the food.

G.B. Foster, *Herbs for Every Garden*, 1966

A cure for children's ailments: hot buttered toast well rubbed with a raw garlic clove.

Czechoslovakia

I have one acquaintance, a close friend and cookbook author, who has for years, as the hay fever season approaches, consumed a daily ration of a dozen cloves of fresh garlic. He chops the garlic finely and sprinkles it on salads, vegetables and meats. Perhaps in self-defense, his wife also participates in this indulgence. My friend advises that he begins this regimen just before the ragweed season begins and before his eyes become 'teary'. Once the season begins it is too late.

Craig Claiborne, *NY Times*, 21 March 1979

In case of deafness, a few drops of garlic juice dropped into the ear have proved beneficial.

Cassell's *Domestic Dictionary* (n.d.)

[In Texas and California] there is a folk belief which says garlic is a cure for cancer of the lungs and leukemia – apparently there is some evidence that concentrated garlic juice can arrest the growth of certain experimentally induced tumours in animals.

W. A. R. Thompson

To cure hysteria in girls: apply garlic juice to their noses.

India

Garlic is called the physic of the peasants, especially in warm countries where it is eaten before going to work in order to guarantee them from the pernicious effects of foul air.

Alexis Soyer

For septicaemia and other eye diseases: the juice from garlic is mixed with betel nut and alum and used as eye drops. (NB: not recommended.)

Malaya

Garlic is very good for cleaning oil paintings. You crush it and use the juice. It's true! it's true! But not the whole painting, only a little corner to see what's what. Only *palliativo*, not cure.

Aldo

A cure for boils: a clove of garlic crushed into warm milk and taken every night for at least a week.

Switzerland

Garlick, held in the palm of the hand, cures toothache.

J. Franckenii, Uppsala, 1750

The people in places where the Simoon is frequent, eat garlic and rub their lips and noses with it when they go out in the heat of the summer, to prevent their suffering from the Simoon.

Mountstuart Elphinstone, 19th-century traveller

Galen praised it as the rustics 'Theriac' or heal-all. Chaucer called it 'poor man's treacle' (Greek, *theriacuus*, antidote) and Discorides prescribed it especially for clearing the voice.

Wm. Bullien, *Book of Simples*, 1562

To make a cough medicine, for curing TB and other lung diseases, boil garlic, macerate, strain it and add honey. Take a handful of it (garlic) and boil it in 2 quarts of spring water until it is a quart. Then strain it and put in a quart of honey by which make a syrup. Take a spoonful of this at a time, and it will infallibly cure any cough, asthma, shortness of breath, etc. Chew raw garlic for insomnia.

Irish folk medicine

A cure for a stubborn cough: soup made from lentils, ginger and garlic.

India

In Anglo-Saxon medicine: use garlic against elf disease (?), as a drink against demonic temptations, a salve for styes, a poultice against swelling.

Y. Lovelock, *The Vegetable Book*, 1972

When my brother and I had whooping cough, we whooped it up in great style. Then mother found the answer. (Whether it came from a neighbor or was handed down from grandma, I don't remember.) The 'answer' to the whooping cough ... guaranteed, you understand ... was to put GARLIC in our shoes. The combination of hot feet and old garlic can't be beaten! For pure unadulterated SMELL, that's it! ... Strange, it sounds like something out of the Middle Ages, yet the garlic cure was actually taking place in our home around the time of World War I.

quoted by Duncan Emrich in *Folklore on the American Land*

Against mad dogs: boil all together bruised rue leaves, garlic, Venice treacle and pewter scrapings in strong ale. Take 9 spoonsful before food on 7 mornings in a row, and give 6 spoonsful to a bitten dog. Also strain and put the mixture directly on the wound.

from a ms dated 1752 in Calthorpe Church,
Lincs, quoted in *Encylopedia of Superstitions*. Only
those died who did not take the mixture after
a mad dog bit most of the inhabitants of the village.

Suggestions for Reading

American Folk Medicine, a Symposium, Berkeley, 1976
Boizot, Peter, *The Pizza Express Cookbook*, London, 1976
Chowdhary, Savitri, *Indian Cooking*, London, 1975
Darby, W. J., *Food: the Gift of Osiris*, London, 1978
David, Elizabeth, *A Book of Mediterranean Food*, London, 1955
Earle, Mrs. C. W., *Pot-pourri from a Surrey Garden*, London, 1899
Fluck, H. and Jasperson-Schib, R., *Medicinal Plants and their Uses*, London, 1976
Greek Herbal of Dioscorides, Oxford, 1934
Grieve, Mrs. M., *A Modern Herbal*, London, 1978
Guerard, Michel, *Cuisine Minceur*, London, 1978
Hawes, F. N., *Dictionary of Useful and Everyday Plants and their Common Names*, Cambridge, 1975
Heaton, Nell, *Cooking Dictionary*, London, 1953
Hehn, V. & Stallybrass, J. S., *Wandering of Plants and Animals from their First Home*, London, 1888
Herklots, G. A. C., *Vegetables in South-East Asia*, London, 1972
Hume, Rosemary and Downes, Muriel, *The Cordon Bleu Book of Jams, Preserves and Pickles*, London, 1972
Jones, H. A., & Mann, L. K., *Onions and their Allies*, London, 1963
Kato, Yoshio, *Garlic, Unknown Miracle Worker*, Amagasakici, 1973
Khayat, M. K. & Keatinge, M. C., *Food from the Arab World*, Lebanon, 1961
Krochmal, A. & C., *Guide to the Medicinal Plants of the United States*, New York, 1973
Leach, M. (ed.), *Standard Dictionary of Folklore, Mythology and Legend*, New York, 1972
Logan, P., *Making the Cure, a Look at Irish Folk Medicine*, London, 1972
Lovelock, Y., *The Vegetable Book of Unnatural History*, London, 1972
Manjon, M. & O'Brien, C., *Spanish Cooking at Home and on Holiday*, London, 1973
Parkinson, J., *The Theatre of Plants*, London, 1640
Pullar, Philippa, *Consuming Passions*, London, 1970
Ray, Elizabeth, *The Best of Eliza Acton*, London, 1968
Rose, Evelyn, *The Complete International Jewish Cookbook*, London, 1978
Simmonds, N. W., *Evolution of Plant Crops*, London, 1976
Soyer, Alexis, *The Pantropheon, or a History of Food and its Preparation in Ancient Times*, reprinted London, 1977
Tannahill, R., *Food in History*, London, 1973
Tenison, Marika Hanbury, *Deep Freeze Sense*, London, 1976
Wilson, C. A., *Food and Drink in Britain*, London, 1973
Yearbook of Agriculture, *Gardening for Food and Fun*, Washington, D.C., 1977

Index to the Recipes

We remember the fish, which we did eat in Egypt freely; the cucumbers, and the melons, and the leeks, and the onions, and the garlick: But now our soul is dried away: there is nothing at all, beside this manna, before our eyes.

Numbers 11:5, 6.